More praise for
TRANSFORMED BY THE LIGHT

"Fascinating . . . Dramatic . . . Startling."
—*The Toledo Blade*

"Breaks new ground."
—*SSC Booknews*

"Fascinating, thought-provoking and highly readable . . . Dr. Morse and Mr. Perry have certainly pursued their research in a methodical, scientific manner."
—*The Montgomery Advertiser*

Also by Melvin Morse, M.D., with Paul Perry
Published by Ivy Books:

CLOSER TO THE LIGHT: Learning from the Near-Death
    Experiences of Children

TRANSFORMED BY THE LIGHT

The Powerful Effect of Near-Death Experiences on People's Lives

Melvin Morse, M.D., with Paul Perry

IVY BOOKS • NEW YORK

Ivy Books
Published by Ballantine Books
Copyright © 1992 by Melvin L. Morse, M.D., and Paul Perry

Library of Congress Catalog Card Number: 92-13205

ISBN 0-8041-1183-9

This edition published by arrangement with Villard Books, a division of Random House, Inc.

Manufactured in the United States of America

First Ballantine Books Edition: February 1994

To my patients in my private practice of medicine.
Only with their support would this
research be possible.

—Melvin Morse

To my wife, Darlene Bennett Perry

—Paul Perry

Preface

What Is a Near-Death Experience?

Millions worldwide have had near-death experiences. By examining thousands of near-death experiences, medical researchers have been able to identify the common stages or elements that define the NDE. There are basically nine traits that characterize this experience, although some researchers analyze NDEs into even more traits to make their research more precise.

To have all nine of the traits is to experience a "full-blown" NDE. Those are rare. Usually a person having an NDE has one or two of the traits: an out-of-body experience and a tunnel experience, for instance. The point is, one does not have to have a full-blown NDE to be transformed by the experience. Many, particularly children, only have the experience of light. Others have only the tunnel experience. These, as well as long and elaborate experiences, are still NDEs. The research presented in this book shows that virtually all of those who have NDEs are transformed by the experience. For instance, they have a greater zest of life and virtually no fear of death. Some are transformed in less visible ways. They have developed psychic abilities and even increased intelligence as a result of their brush with death.

The nine essential traits of NDEs are listed below. Each trait is illustrated by an actual story of someone who has returned from death's door:

1. A Sense of Being Dead

"It was hard to explain. It was a time when I was not the wife of my husband, I was not the parent of my children, I was not the child of my parents. I was totally and completely me."

—A 65-year-old Chicago woman after a cardiac arrest

2. Peace and Painlessness

"It was as though the ribbons that bind me to the world had been cut. I no longer felt fear nor did I feel my body, for that matter. I could hear them (doctors and nurses) working around me but it meant nothing."

—A Georgia housewife who "died" after an auto wreck

3. Out-of-Body Experience

"I was able to look down at myself in my hospital bed. There were doctors and nurses moving busily around me. I could see them roll a machine into the room and put it near the foot of my bed. It had two handles sticking out of a kind of box. I found out later that it was one of those machines they use to shock the heart and get it started when it has stopped.

"A priest came in and began to give me last rites. I moved down to the bottom of the bed and watched everything that was going on. It was like being in the audience at a play.

"Behind me in the bed was a clock. It was up on the wall. I could see both myself in the bed and the clock, which read 11:11 A.M.

"Then I went back into my body. I remember waking up and looking for myself at the foot of the bed."

> —An Arizona woman who nearly died from
> a reaction to medication

4. Tunnel Experience

"I was playing golf as a storm was brewing when—wham—I got hit by a bolt of lightning. I hovered above my body for a few seconds and then I felt myself being sucked up this tunnel. I couldn't see anything around me, but I had a sense of moving forward very rapidly. I was clearly in a tunnel and knew it when I saw this light at the other end getting bigger and bigger."

> —A Southern car dealer after being struck by lightning

5. People of Light

"I was met at the end of the tunnel by a bunch of people. They were all glowing from the inside like lanterns. The whole place was glowing in the same way, like everything in it was filled with light. I didn't know any of the people I met there, but they all seemed to love me very much."

—A 10-year-old boy who experienced a cardiac arrest

6. Being of Light

"I remember waking up in a garden filled with large flowers. If I had to describe them, I would say they looked like big dahlias. It was warm and light in this garden and it was beautiful.

"I looked around the garden and there was this Being. The garden was extraordinarily beautiful, but everything paled in his presence. I felt completely loved and completely nourished by him. It was the most delightful feeling I've ever known. Although it was several years ago, I can still feel that feeling."

—A middle-aged woman describing her childhood NDE

7. Life Review

"This Being of Light surrounded me and showed me my life. Everything you do is there for you to evaluate. As unpleasant as some parts of it are for you to see, it feels so good to get it all out. I remember one particular incident in this review when, as a child, I yanked my little sister's Easter basket away from her, because there was a toy in it that I wanted. Yet in the review, I felt her feelings of disappointment and loss and rejection.

"I was the very people I hurt and I was the very people that I helped to feel good."

—An Ohio woman who had a near-death experience at age 23

8. Reluctance to Return

"After the review of my life I didn't want to return to my body. I was comfortable there, and the light that surrounded me was pure love. He (the Being of Light) asked me if I wanted to go back and I said, 'No.' He then told me I had to go back, that there was more work to be done. I was then sucked back into my body. There was no other way to describe it. Suddenly I was lying there, looking up at a doctor with paddles in his hand.

"For a moment I was angry at being brought back to life. 'Don't ever do that to me again!' I said. It was a shock to my friend who had worked so hard to save me."

—A cardiologist who was resuscitated by one of his peers

9. Personality Transformation

"The first thing I saw when I awoke in the hospital was a flower, and I cried. Believe it or not, I had never really seen a flower until I came back from death. One thing I learned when I died was that we are all part of one big, living universe. If we think we can hurt another person or another living thing without hurting ourselves, we are sadly mistaken."

—A 62-year-old businessman after surviving a cardiac arrest

ACKNOWLEDGMENTS

The Seattle study is to my knowledge the largest study of near-death experiences to date. The immense amount of work and the hundreds of people who contributed cannot ever be properly acknowledged. I would like to thank every participant in the study, especially the control patients who had to fill out long questionnaires for no reason apparent to them. I hope that after reading this book, every subject who contributed will be proud to have been a part of the Seattle study.

I would like to thank my research mentors, Archie Bleyer, M.D., and Jerrold Milstein, M.D. Whenever I felt stuck or needed inspiration, I would reflect on conversations I have had with them. John Neff, M.D., was a constant source of emotional support and inspiration. Edgar Marcuse, M.D., intervened at a crucial time in my life as he has done so many times in the past. I would like to thank the nursing staff of both Children's Hospital and Valley Medical Center for their invaluable insights.

I would like to thank Rich Roodman and Jim Distlehorst and the administration of Valley Medical Center for their unflagging support of my research. The knowledge that I had the complete support of my hospital and medical staff made many a chilly wind that much easier to bear. My work is undeniably controversial and the support of such men as John Neff and Jim Distlehorst has helped me to focus on my research and not the controversy it generates.

I could not have found the time to be a busy pediatrician and write without the generous support of my partners. Margaret Clements, M.D., always provides intellectual inspiration at just the right moment. David Christopher, Gary German, Garciella Del Rio, Margaret Clements, and Mike Anderson are superb physicians and outstanding human beings and I could not have finished this second book without their help. I would also like to thank my office staff for handling the thousands of phone calls and tiny pieces of paper that yet another appearance on television seemed to generate. My office nurse, MaryAnne Anderson, keeps me firmly grounded on planet Earth and is the real secret to my success in practice.

I would like to thank my attorney Stew Cogan for all of his help. He is cheaper than a psychiatrist and far more practical. This book could not have happened without the trust that Villard Books has had in me. I want to thank Diane Reverand for her merciless job of editing, my writer Paul Perry, who has a great gift of making the incomprehensible understandable, and my agent Nat Sobel and others in his office, especially Craig Holden. I feel lucky that I am not simply an author, but a member of a great team dedicated to furthering our understanding of near-death experiences and their impact on our society.

The actual study itself was largely the result of Shannon Greer's efforts. She handled all aspects of the study, from designing questionnaires and interviewing, to the tedious hours of organizing details and data collection. I have been greatly influenced by the writings and thinking of Vernon Neppe, M.D., and feel he is the premier researcher in the area of consciousness research today. The study was completed with the assistance of the International Association of Near-Death Studies, and I would like to thank the Seattle chapter for their support, as I have been affiliated with them for over ten years. Kim Clark and Bruce Greyson have known me since I was a callow Fellow at Seattle Children's Hospital when I first blundered into this field. Any sensitivity and insight I have into the psychology of those who have had near-death experiences or pre-death visions is due to their help.

There are so many others who have helped me. Many have written letters that I have read and been influenced by, but never had time to respond to. I have met some after lectures, or on radio talk shows, or at the airport. All have contributed and I thank you.

I dedicated my first book to my wife Allison, and she is the source of all of my inspiration. Our marriage is a true partnership and all that I have accomplished could have only occurred with her help. I thank my children Bridget, Colleen, and Brett for their patience and love. My youngest son, Cody, may have contributed more than anyone else for thoughtfully waking me up at night to remind me to finish one more chapter. Finally, I thank my mother, for everything.

CONTENTS

Preface   vii
Acknowledgments   xiii

1 The Transformed   1
2 The Transformations Study   29
3 Not Afraid to Live—or Die   64
4 Seeing with the Mind   89
5 Believing the Unseen   116
6 The Circuit Boards of Mysticism   139
7 The Transformations Artifacts   170
8 The Glow of God   203

Appendix   239
Bibliography   245
Selected Bibliography of Papers and Periodicals 257

1

The Transformed

"It is worth dying to find out what life is."

—*T. S. Eliot*

"In honesty, Dr. Morse, I don't think the experience has changed me at all."

I had just finished listening to Donna tell the frightening story of the night she almost died and was now trying to find out if she had noticed any changes in the three years since her near-death experience.

Her story was typical of the hundreds of near-death experiences I have heard in the last five years, but it still sent electric chills up my spine to hear her tell it in such a matter-of-fact way.

When Donna was twelve she came down with an acute case of pneumonia. She was allowed to stay at home, since her doctor thought he had it controlled with medication. Her orders were the standard ones for this infection: take the medicine, drink a lot of fluids, and get plenty of rest. She was doing all of those things on this particular evening when bad turned to worse and almost became fatal.

As Donna tells it, she was watching television from the couch in her Cincinnati, Ohio, home when she found it difficult to catch her breath. She tried not to think about it, concentrating instead on the sitcom that was blaring on the screen. Soon, it felt as though a metal band had tightened around her chest, crushing the very wind out of her.

Donna screamed for her mother.

What her mother saw when she came into the room must have been frightening because she grabbed Donna and pulled her outside to get some fresh air. Donna went down on all fours in the front yard, gasping for air on this cold winter night. Her lungs tightened up and breathing became impossible. Donna's mother acted quickly. She scooped her daughter into the car and raced for the hospital. The last thing Donna heard was her mother screaming her name. Then reality changed radically:

"I remember seeing a light. I was curious and drawn to it. It was like looking into the flash of a camera—white, goldish and very bright.

"Suddenly hands were reaching to me and I saw my grandparents. The hands and my grandparents weren't just part of the light, they were the light. There were hundreds of hands, hands everywhere. They looked like Greek sculpture and they waved me on toward my grandparents who had been dead for several years.

"I communicated with my grandparents but I didn't talk. I don't even remember thinking. But I was right there with them as they spoke. What did they say? They said I had solved most of my problems and could now go either way. That meant I could either stay with them in the light or go back to my body. It was up to me and it wasn't absolutely necessary to stay with them."

Donna doesn't remember making a decision but she came back. When she did, she got a dose of medical reality. The physician who treated her at the hospital said her "hallucination" had been caused by drugs. Since he had given her none at the hospital, he wanted to know what type of drugs she was taking on her own.

Her pediatrician said the same thing. When Donna and her mom told her doctor about the experience of light she said that it must have been caused by some kind of hallucinatory drug. "Otherwise," said the pediatrician, "you're saying that she had a near-death experience!"

After listening to Donna's story, I thought that was exactly what she'd had. She certainly had many of the elements as we near-death researchers know them. She went from intense pain to having a sense of peace and painlessness. She was engulfed by an intense light filled with love that drew her to it. She saw people of light—in this case her deceased grandparents—who comforted her with the knowledge that everything was all right. She was given a chance to return to her body (which she had no sense of during the experience) or stay in the light with her grandparents. Now she was facing medical disbelief, the unofficial symptom, in which doctors were trying to tell her that this experience did not really happen. In short, they were telling her to deny her own reality.

That is where I came in. I was at a medical conference and was introduced to Donna by a colleague. She had read my previous book, *Closer to the Light*, and wanted to talk to someone in the medical profession who could "understand."

I understood her situation very well. Having talked to hundreds of children and adults about their near-death experiences I know the disbelief they face from many doctors who have difficulty admitting that some things can't be explained by medical manuals.

In talking to all of these near-death experiencers, I had come to believe something else as well: they are all transformed by this experience of light. The notion that NDEers are transformed by their experience is not a new one. It is just that no one had conducted a systematic study with proper controls to see if people are transformed.

Some researchers have gone so far as to state that one cannot have had a "real" NDE unless one is transformed by it. Phyllis Atwater, for instance, says that the aftereffects of the NDE are the yardstick for its authenticity.

With my own patients I have seen this transformation take many forms. Sometimes the person who has a near-death experience becomes more loving and caring. Sometimes they have remarkable insights into areas they previously knew nothing about. Sometimes they have become downright psychic, able to see the future in their dreams or accurately predict events through intuition.

But for how long? People who have relatives who died of lung cancer often say that they are transformed by the experience and quit smoking. But when they are surveyed a few months later, they are smoking again.

For how long are NDEers transformed?

Although no one had conducted a study to examine the actual transformations that occur, I was certain from my own experiences that every person who has an NDE is transformed in some way.

Which is why I asked Donna the question: "So how has this experience changed your life?"

And why I was puzzled by her reply: *"In honesty, Dr. Morse, I don't think the experience has changed me at all."*

I began to probe deeper. Maybe your relationship with your parents is better? "Not really. It's always been pretty good." Perhaps you're smarter in school, I suggested. She thought about it a minute and shook her head, "no." Okay, your ability to do math has improved? "Not hardly," she said. I was patient, knowing that children and teenagers often don't think they are changed by the experience.

"Can you see the future?" I asked.

She looked slightly uncomfortable. "Oh that," she said. "Who told you?"

Without further prompting, Donna began telling tales of precognitive dreams, ones that warn of events soon to come. In all she could remember four such dreams that fit into the category of "verifiable psychic experiences," which means they are dreams she told others about *before* the events in the dream occurred.

For instance she dreamed that her grandfather died

only a few days before he did so, very unexpectedly. The nature of these dreams was quite interesting. Four nights in a row, Donna dreamed vividly that her grandfather went to the family grave plot and cleaned the spot on the stone where his name would be engraved. Then he sat at the grave site and talked to his grandson who had previously died in an automobile accident. She couldn't hear what he was saying in any of the dreams, but she told her mother after each one that she somehow knew he was going to die.

He died of a massive heart attack just a few days after her fourth dream.

After the grandfather's death, Donna's mother read his journal. He wrote of sweeping off the grave site and talking to his grandson on the very days that Donna dreamed it.

She told me of other such dreams.

In one disturbing example, Donna dreamed she was at a party with a friend. Tickets were being handed out with writing on them. Donna couldn't remember the one she received, but on her friend's was written the word *suicide*. She told her family about the dream at the breakfast table the next morning and didn't think much more about it until she was at a party with the friend about a week later. There her friend began talking about family problems. She mentioned a desire to commit suicide.

A couple of days later, Donna suddenly had a premonition that her friend's threat was coming true. It didn't come in the form of a dream or a vision, said Donna, just a strong sense that this good friend was trying to take her life. In a state of panic, Donna rushed to her friend's house. She found her there slitting her wrists in the bathroom! Through Donna's intervention the girl was able to get psychiatric help. Both her dream and premonition had come true.

There were other psychic dreams as well. She and a friend had shared a dream while the friend was away at summer camp. Another time she dreamed the contents of a letter and was able to tell its contents to the person who wrote it while the letter was still in the mail. In another event, best described as a vision, she was on a hike in the mountains where she saw a friend being followed by a shadow. She shouted for her friend to look out and as she did a rock ledge beneath the friend's feet crumbled. She feels that her intervention saved her friend from a climbing accident. Based on her track record I have no doubt that she was probably right.

DIFFERENT "DEATHS," COMMON TRAITS

"So it looks like your near-death experience *has* changed things for you," I said. She laughed and acknowledged that it had. Donna, like all the others, had been transformed.

The interest created by *Closer to the Light* brought to me hundreds of people who had had near-death experiences. Most were adults who had had their brush with death as children. There were people who had nearly drowned and those who had been struck by speeding automobiles. There were people who had "died" having their tonsils taken out as well as those who had stuck their heads in plastic bags and nearly suffocated. Some had gone into respiratory collapse from reaction to penicillin. A couple had been clobbered into comas by baseball bats. One was even struck in the ear by lightning as she spoke on the telephone during a thunderstorm.

They had nearly died in very different ways. After talking with them, I realized they had one important thing in common. *They were transformed.*

Virtually everyone to whom I spoke had little or no fear of death. Even though their near-death experience may have happened several decades ago, they were not concerned about dying. Why? Because they *knew* something, a message that came from the light which almost all of them saw. As one ten-year-old girl told me, "It was like I had a new life. I'm not afraid so much of dying because I know more about it now."

A zest for life was present in all of them, too. By this I mean that they pursue everything life has to offer. They just want to squeeze every drop they can out of life. Sometimes they are not even aware of this very fundamental change in their attitude. As one woman in her seventies said to me: "It would be a waste of time to interview me, since my near-death experience had no effect whatsoever on my life. Besides, I don't have time to be interviewed. I'm too busy with gardening, volunteer work, and my part-time job. There's nothing special about me at all."

Low death anxiety and a zest for life were common traits in the people with whom I spoke. From the many people who contacted me I discovered differences that went beyond just changes in attitude.

A large number of people claimed transformations that were paranormal. Some claimed that they had achieved much higher intelligence after their near-death experiences. One, a snowplow operator in upstate New York with the all-American name of Tom Sawyer, found himself writing a string of numbers and symbols within a year of his experience. He didn't know why he wrote them or what they meant, but he frequently found himself doodling during coffee breaks or in the evening after work. When he showed these musings to a college professor he found that he was writing the equations of Max Plank, a physicist, who contributed much of what we know today about atomic theory. Sawyer now says that his near-death experience was a "short course in nuclear physics." But why and how did a person with a high school education get such information? Was it from the light?

Others were certain they had developed psychic abilities. They, like Donna, could now tell what was going to happen in the future. One woman was so disturbed by her ability to see into the future that she had herself medicated, after having a prophetic dream about her brother's murder by intruders. For nearly five years she took prescription drugs that dulled her senses and kept her from being psychic. Finally, tired of a dulled life, she quit the drugs and has now accepted that she will know the outcome of some events before they happen. Why was she privileged, or perhaps cursed, to have such information?

I noticed many other changes as time went on. Some were very profound, as in those people with the increased intelligence or newfound psychic abilities. Others were very subtle. For example, many cannot wear watches because "something" keeps breaking them.

Some of these people reported "guardian angels" who stayed with them long after the frightening experience of almost dying. I was fascinated by the help they received from these merciful companions.

The more I spoke to these people, the more fascinated I became and thought that this was worthy of scientific investigation. After hearing Olaf Sunden's story, I decided to study this legion of the transformed as closely as I could.

A CASE STUDY IN KNOWLEDGE

The way in which Olaf Sunden almost died was simple enough. What happened after the experience of his near death is too complex for me to comprehend.

At the age of fourteen, Olaf had his tonsils removed. During a routine surgical procedure, he was overdosed on ether, a frequent occurrence in those days when ether was administered drop by drop onto a cotton cloth placed close to the patient's face. Olaf stopped breathing and his panicked surgeon began to shake him. His heart may well have stopped at this point, too. Although he was technically comatose, Olaf had a sense of being dead. As he wrote in a very dramatic report:

"Suddenly I rolled into a ball and seemed to smash into a wall into another reality. The passage from this side to the other was extremely painful, a suffocation. The forces which brought me through the death barrier were terrific and the boundary-barrier was extremely strong.

"Suddenly I was on the other side, and all pains were gone. I had lost all my interest and attachment to my biological life.

[I realized that] the boundary between life and death is a strange creation of our mind. It is horrifying and real when perceived from this side [the side of the living] and yet is insignificant when perceived from the other side.

"My first impression was a total surprise. How could I exist in such a comfortable way, and how could I perceive and think while being dead, and yet have no body?"

Olaf felt as though he were floating in "a universe with no boundaries." He saw the universe as a system of shrinking soap bubbles, one in which the bubbles appeared in spherical, concentric trains that moved in intricate patterns that he completely comprehended.

On the verge of death, this fourteen-year-old boy with a mediocre school record felt as though he had been handed the keys to the universe. "I felt I had a total comprehension which made everything understandable," he wrote. In his near-death experience, Olaf stood at a "bright orange light." He called this light "the point of annihilation," a frightening place to be but one that gave him universal understanding.

Although Olaf wanted to stay with the light, he felt his "mind splitting into two parts" with that portion that understood everything being left behind. He saw it disappear above him as a beautiful bright galaxy of light, while he was forced into a tunnel and back to his body. "I remember thinking, 'please let me understand this new physics of relativity,' " wrote Olaf. "Then I felt a bump and was caught in a channel and transported with tremendous force back into my body. I collected all my power to remember the cosmic comprehension of the universal machinery."

Olaf's cosmic journey ended in an illuminated operating theater where he awoke to find himself surrounded by broken glass and scattered instruments, four frantic physicians and several upset nurses. Two years later he learned that he still had his tonsils left, they had never been removed as planned.

The near-death experience immediately changed Olaf's character. He went from being an average student to one who was arrogant and even heretical, refusing explanations presented at school in search of his own. He used theories he had learned on "the other side" to explain the work of Albert Einstein.

Olaf at first felt that the near-death experience was little more than an extraordinary dream. As he progressed to the honors program from being a student who seemed learning disabled, he realized that something had happened in the course of his cosmic adventure.

Still he did not truly trust his vision until the early sixties, when he was in his mid-forties. It was then, when the discovery of the neutrino was made public, that Olaf realized that his near-death insights were correct. A neutrino is a type of nuclear particle that is able to pass through the massive core of a star without being altered or affected in any way. When Olaf read about neutrinos he realized that they were among the particles he saw in his experience, the "soap bubbles" that passed through solid bodies.

Now he believed that his near-death experience gave him tremendous insight into the nature of the universe. Some mysterious source of intelligence had been tapped. He was smarter than before, but also free from thinking that confined him to accepted theories and values.

Proof of this increased intelligence lies in his many technical accomplishments, most of which occurred as a result of his trusting the intuition that came to him as a result of the near-death experience. He now refers to his near fatal tonsillectomy as "my cosmic gift."

Olaf holds about a hundred chemical patents, discoveries that made him one of the top engineers in the research and development field. He discovered a way of including more chalk in making paper. Paper is made primarily from wood pulp derived from chopped-up trees. With his highly developed scientific vision, Olaf discovered a way to add 25 percent more chalk or kaolin to the paper without changing its quality in any way. That discovery translates into roughly 25 percent fewer trees having to be cut down to supply our paper needs.

Olaf cites another piece of evidence when proving the validity of his "cosmic gift." Twenty-five years ago his teenage daughter sustained severe head injuries in an automobile accident. She was in a coma for three months and doctors predicted she was likely to stay that way. They frankly told Olaf that his daughter would exist in a vegetative state for the rest of her life.

In this desperate situation, Olaf's near-death experience came to his and his daughter's help. He had to accept the neurological diagnosis, but he did not accept that all possibilities to an acceptable life were exhausted. He supposed that his daughter was on the other side and in a situation like that in which he was after the ether suffocation. He remembered how his own memory of swimming along with the sea waves appeared like a key that opened up the tunnel for his return to life. Perhaps such a memory from life could also be the key to his daughter's return. Fortunately, Olaf was in possession of a medical substance, a strange relative to caffeine, that he had successfully tested on himself and on his daughter in order to improve their memories during both scientific lectures and school examinations.

Olaf decided to make a final desperate experiment with this substance. The first test, seven weeks after the accident, gave a dramatic effect. The unconscious, inactive girl tried to rise up from the bed for fifteen minutes but then fell back in total coma again. A second test was made a week later with a much stronger result. When the doctors were called, they confirmed that the coma, against all odds, was reversing, even if any mental contact could not be established for sure. A development toward life had begun, and after a month the girl became conscious. She could then, by pressing the hand, answer mathematical questions. One month after the awakening she was examined in mathematics and passed her student examination, that she otherwise would have failed. It took her three years to learn to walk again, and two painful eye operations were required to get the eyes in parallel positions. She is now an architect and mother to two children but still suffers from paralysis in one leg when walking.

To Olaf, this tragic story is an indication that "cosmic gifts" of this kind should be given serious scientific attention.

* * *

Olaf learned about my work from such medical journals as *Lancet*, and *The American Journal of Diseases in Children*. He then read *Closer to the Light* before writing me a letter. Could he come from his home in Sweden to visit? I told him I would be honored.

We met in Washington, D.C., at the International Conference on Near-Death Experiences. Olaf is a tall man in his early seventies. Gray and distinguished, he was the dynamic sort of man who would seem more at home at an ambassador's residence than at a meeting of near-death experiencers. Yet Olaf was delighted to find so many people like himself, people who had gained special insight into life by passing briefly through death's door.

We went to dinner at a French restaurant in Georgetown. Olaf conversed easily with the waiter in French. After ordering a fine bottle of wine, he got to the point of his visit.

"I no longer think I am crazy or a crank because of what happened," said Olaf. "I know that my experience was real and not a fantastic dream. But the question I have is this: Did that knowledge come from inside my own brain or did it come from someplace else? And this universe that I entered. Did I really go to an altered reality?"

RAINBOW REVELATIONS

Was Olaf's experience real?

Did he really gain knowledge through a near-death experience that led him to create more than a hundred formulas so unique that he could have them patented?

When these questions were asked, Olaf calmly and emphatically said, "These death experiences represent a step upwards on the evolutionary ladder. That is the reason why ... a criminal youngster may become social after such an experience. He has taken a step upwards."

The life of Olaf Sunden fired my curiosity about the long-term effects of these experiences, but his case alone did not lead to the Transformations study. I noticed that people were transformed in many different ways, all of them interesting and most of them highly noticeable.

Take James, for instance. He is a black teenager from the projects of East St. Louis who by his own admission should be caught up in the gang violence and drug trade in which most of his friends are involved. Despite the constant peer pressure to do the wrong things, James is on a straight and narrow path because of a near-death experience that occurred when he was nine.

I'll let James tell his own story in his own words:

"I was like nine or ten years old. I don't know how to swim. I was in the peanut pool with my cousins when all of a sudden I was going down. I struggled to breathe and then I just couldn't do it no more. Then I thought I was dreaming. I could see myself. It was like I was looking at me. I felt scared. Then I just floated out of my body into a safe place. It was all bright. I felt peaceful.

"And you know, when I floated out of my body and saw myself, suddenly I realized that we are all the same. There ain't no black and there ain't no white. I saw that bright light and I knew it was all the colors there were, everything was in that light—everything good for me, that is."

James was pulled from the pool by his mother and revived by lifeguards. He embarrassed his mother by crying, "I saw you, I saw you take me out of the pool." At
home he told her about leaving his body and the rainbow revelation that he received in the light. She was
disturbed by what she heard. "Don't talk that trash," she
scolded.

James changed almost immediately after the experience. He quit hanging around with his usual friends because they were already becoming involved in selling
drugs. To his mother's surprise (and relief) he became
serious about school.

Now, eight years after he almost drowned, James is
still serious about school. And his mother still thinks he
is talking trash. I met James through a kind and sensitive teacher at his school. She had read *Closer to the
Light* and realized that the "trash" James was talking
was nothing more or less than a near-death experience.
James was relieved to be able to put a name on the
main event of his life.

"I always thought that I had a dream. Then when I heard
about these near-death experiences I knew that I'd had one. I
feel better about myself. I know that I am different. I don't
think about putting people down for fun like I used to.

"You know, when I left my body I didn't think that I could
come back. The fact that I could really change my attitude
amazed me. I see life the way it really is. It is not meant to be
played with. I don't want to end up here with all this gang violence and poverty. I believe in God very much. I believe God
took me out of my body and kept me in a very safe place
when I almost drowned."

* * *

I was deeply moved when he told me what the long-term effects of his near-death experience were. "Life is not to be played with. I want to better myself."

Although very different people, both Olaf and James were given unique insights into life. For Olaf, it was a deep understanding of molecular chemistry. For James, it was the discovery that skin color is meaningless when compared to the contribution we can make in life.

Each had experiences which changed them greatly from their peers. Despite the extreme difficulty of suddenly becoming a different person, the change appeared to be a comfortable and permanent one. About his switch from a gang member to a ghetto scholar, James said: "Sure it ain't easy. But I ain't going to be like those other people now that I've seen the light."

Is it the light that transforms? I wondered. *Is it the light of the near-death experience that gives people a zest for life, takes away their fear of death and fills them with a sort of goodness?*

There were more questions that begged answers that only a transformations study could answer. *Does the light stay with some people long after their near-death experience is over? Does it come back to them in a seemingly human form?*

GUARDIAN WRITER

I ask this question because of the peculiar case of David G—, a bestselling author.

David lives in Arizona near my co-author Paul Perry.

When he moved into the neighborhood, Paul paid him a visit and gave him a copy of our book as a "get-acquainted" gift. A few days later Paul received a surprising call from David. "I had one of these as a kid," he said. "It changed my life completely."

David's story is simple and straightforward. It's the aftereffects that are puzzling.

"I had infectious hepatitis and my temperature had reached 104 degrees. I was extremely sick and was in my bed at home. My mother was standing beside the bed with my father and the doctor was there too. He had just rigged up an IV bottle and put a line into a vein in my arm.

"I was wide awake and listening to them talk about my case. I remember the doctor telling my mother that I was very sick but that she shouldn't worry because a lot of kids get this sick and pull through. Suddenly I noticed a fourth person in the room. There was a woman in the corner, behind my parents!

"At the same time I saw her I realized that I was out of my body! I was suddenly across the room with this woman and able to see the backs of my parents and look back on myself lying there in bed!

"I turned toward the woman. She was beckoning me to come to her. I think she was blonde and she was certainly very pleasant. She was also very bright and hard to look at.

"As quickly as I left my body I was back in it. I could still see her behind my parents, trying to get me to come to her. I sat up in bed and reached for her and my arms passed right through her. I would have fallen out of bed if my father had not grabbed me. As it was I think I knocked over the IV bottle.

"I told them about the woman in the corner but she was gone by the time they looked and they couldn't have seen her anyway. She was for my eyes only."

The experience immediately changed David. He became very introverted. Rather than spend much time with other friends, David was happy in the play world he created. He also stopped being materialistic. For a child of nine, this meant he no longer wanted all the toys being marketed on television. He watched very little television. The experience with the "guardian angel" (which is what he now called the woman of light) had made David a happy loner.

The guardian angel remained for David's mind only. She has never appeared to him again. Yet during periods of stress when he needs comfort, the woman of light is there. He can feel her presence in the room, although he can't see her.

Perhaps the most mysterious thing about David's guardian angel is her effect on his work. David says there are times when he is writing that the guardian angel helps him. At a particularly difficult point in a story, when he has mulled over his plot from every possible angle and can't find a way to proceed, the unseen hand of the guardian angel takes over and guides him through his work.

"It is almost like automatic writing, I don't know how else to describe it," says David. "Sometimes there are large sections of my writing that I don't remember having produced. Even my wife, who works closely with me, doesn't recognize this writing as being my own. She says, 'this doesn't look like your style,' and I have to agree with that. There are sections of my book that seem to have come to me from somewhere else."

The experience of the light changed David, like Olaf and James, and seemed to bring him greater direction and insight, but his light took the form of a guardian angel. As I thought of David's experiences, I had to ask myself:

Are there many guardian angels among the transformed? Is it the long-term presence of these "angels" that accounts for the lifelong transformation that most near-death experiencers have?

THE GENESIS OF RESEARCH

Questions, questions, questions.

The stories of these four remarkable people as well as the hundreds of others who contacted me after the publication of *Closer to the Light* just led to more questions than there were answers. I was reminded of what was said to me by Dr. Archie Bleyer, my mentor from my research days: "Watch out, Mel. Good research always poses more questions than it provides answers."

I found his warning to be true, especially when it comes to the field of near-death studies. I decided to undertake another major study into the nature of the near-death experience. This time I wanted to examine the ways in which this experience changes the people who have it. Before planning this study, a massive one to be sure, I thought about the events that led to the Seattle study, the ground-breaking research that became the framework for *Closer to the Light*.

That earlier work began innocently enough.

In 1982 as a pediatric resident I was examining one of my patients, a little girl named Katie, who had almost drowned in a community pool in Idaho. Even without her near-death experience Katie was a remarkable story. She was documented as not having a pulse for nineteen minutes. When I first saw her, her pupils were fixed and dilated, meaning that irreversible brain damage had most likely occurred.

I worked hard on her anyway, although in my heart I didn't think she would survive.

Her family had other ideas. She had a large family and over the course of the next three days there were always family members surrounding her bed, holding her hands, talking to her, or praying. Sometimes they did all three at once, which made things a little more chaotic in intensive care than the doctors and nurses wanted. Still we put up with it, partly because the family just refused to leave, but mainly because we thought she was going to die.

I remember putting a line into one of Katie's arteries and having bright red blood spurt across her bedsheets. As this was happening, her entire family had joined hands around the bed and were praying. Let them do it, I said to myself. She's dead anyway.

Three days later she made a full recovery.

One afternoon I casually asked her what she remembered about being in the pool. I was trying to figure out why she had nearly drowned, thinking perhaps that she hit her head on the pool's edge or maybe even had an epileptic fit. But the answer that she gave wasn't anything like I expected: "Do you mean when I saw the heavenly father?"

Over the next few days Katie told her remarkable story. While in the hospital she had left her comatose body and was now able to describe in detail the doctors who treated her and what it was that they did.

She then described going up a long, dark tunnel where she was greeted by a golden-haired "angel" named Elizabeth. The angel took her hand and said, "I am here to help you."

For the next three days the angel did just that. She calmed Katie and even took her on a voyage back to her home, where she was able to see one of her brothers play with his toys in his bedroom and watch as her mother cooked a hurried meal before rushing back to the hospital to be at her bedside.

Not knowing what else to say, I asked her what it was like "up there."

"You'll see, Dr. Morse," she said. "Heaven is fun."

Katie's case defied conventional neurology. According to the textbooks in the field, a child with Katie's symptoms should have the absence of any brain function and therefore should comprehend nothing. As one of the top textbooks in the field says, coma should "wipe clean the slate of human consciousness."

Katie's experience (as well as others, as I was soon to find out) did not fit neatly into the textbooks of neurology.

I began to examine the medical literature on near-death experiences and was not happy with the quality of research. Although it was interesting, it seemed to be largely anecdotal, just a collection of interesting stories. With few exceptions that's the way the research was.

Even Dr. Raymond Moody agreed. In his groundbreaking book *Life After Life*, he acknowledged that his research was not scientific, but a collection of stories. He openly challenged the medical and scientific community to research near-death experiences. He boldly asserted that if such studies were done, it would confirm his assertion that near-death experiences are the same for all human beings at the point of death.

I accepted Dr. Moody's challenge. I conducted the Seattle study at Children's Hospital in Seattle. There my colleagues and I studied twenty-six children who had survived cardiac arrest. We compared their experiences of nearly dying to those of 176 seriously ill children who did not experience clinical death. The two groups were carefully matched in terms of ages, sex, medications, and anesthetics used. All were subjected to the frightening environment of the intensive-care unit. Both groups had had the same lack of oxygen to the brain (as documented by blood tests) and the same general blood chemistry.

Almost all of the clinically dead patients had one or more elements of the near-death experience. Yet not one of the 176 "control" patients had any symptoms resembling a near-death experience.

What did this study show? Quite simply that thinking or feeling as if you are going to die is not enough to cause a near-death experience. Near death is actually required before one has the core symptoms of an NDE. In a nutshell, the core experience is the sensation of leaving the physical body, entering into a world of darkness followed by experiencing a warm and loving light. The experience of the light, which is most commonly described by children, is a light "full of good things," as one of our young study volunteers described it.

The Seattle study proved that one needs to be "near death" to have a "near-death experience," and that the NDE is not a fantasy caused by resuscitation. It also proved that NDEs are not a fantasy or hallucination, since none of the control group had them. Surprisingly, no one had ever researched this most basic question.

I discovered many things by conducting the Seattle study, but the most important thing I learned was to listen. Yes, listen. By listening to the wisdom of these children I realized we can begin to learn about the Greatest Mystery, the one that has puzzled humankind since the beginning: *What happens to us when we die?*

TRANSFORMATION STUDY QUESTIONS

Now I was about to launch a study that involved an entirely different question: *What happens to near-death experiencers who do not die?* How are their lives transformed?

I took a large pad of paper from a cupboard and found a quiet spot to sit in the living room. At the top of the page I wrote "Transformations." Underneath it: "A study to determine the ways in which near-death experiences change people."

One by one, I listed the questions that this study would answer:

Do NDEers really have decreased death anxiety? They seem to have a lesser fear of death than people who have not had NDEs. Is their fear really less, or does it just seem to be less? It has been assumed that NDEers do not fear death like the rest of us, but, in looking at the scientific literature, I discovered that no researchers had done an extensive study of death anxiety.

I jotted down a Woody Allen quote that stuck in my mind: "Only three things are certain: Death, taxes, and fear of both of them." Was it possible that NDEers feared only one of these?

Do NDEers really have an increase in psychic abilities? Many of the people I deal with claim that their near-death experience has led to psychic events. These are not eccentric people who dress funny and read tea leaves or fool around with Ouija boards. These are bankers or housewives who look as if they just stepped out of "The Donna Reed Show." They are ordinary people who have had something out of the ordinary happen to them.

Two people came to mind as I jotted down this question: one a banker and the other a housewife.

First the banker and his dream that came true:

"I had a dream of a man I knew who appeared for a second in the middle of the night, dressed in a black suit, standing as if his feet were on a cloud. I had not seen him in ten years.

"The following day I approved a check at the bank where I work for a man who was related to the man in the dream. I asked him about the man and learned that he had died the night before."

The banker was actually comforted by this experience. He said that it confirmed for him a spiritual side to the universe, one that gave him a sense that there is more to life than meets the eye.

The housewife's psychic experience was just as remarkable:

"I happened to touch one of my son's friends on the arm when I suddenly had a vivid, visual image of blood spurting from his shoulder and the arm falling off! I pulled away and gasped in horror. I had to blink several times before the vision went away.

"That evening I told my husband what I had seen. The next day it came true. The boy lost his arm in an industrial accident."

This experience was very disturbing for the housewife. Unlike the banker, she found no comfort in knowing events before they happened. My findings indicate that there is often no comfort in being psychic for many NDEers.

Why do NDEers have a greater zest for living than the normal population? All of the near-death experiencers with whom I spoke have a desire to get everything they can out of life. Many describe themselves as "workaholics," yet few of them seem to have the negative aspects of being type-A, such as the anger that often comes with the person who wants nothing to get in his way.

We wanted to know their spiritual values and how they live their lives. Do they really spend more time with their families? Do they have more hobbies? Do they spend more time in meditation? These are the footprints of the near-death experience, proof that the changes in these people are real.

Said one NDEer: "There's a pun intended when I say that I've seen the light. I know now that life is for living and that light is for later."

Do NDEers really achieve a higher intelligence? Olaf Sunden and Tom Sawyer are but two of many who claim to have an increased intelligence after their near-death experience. Could this be possible? Do they tap into a higher source of intelligence from *outside* their brains (as Olaf wondered) or does this extraordinary experience activate a portion of their brains never before used?

This is an exciting question and reminded me of a metaphysical quote from none other than Albert Einstein: "The greatest experience we can have is the mysterious."

I put the notepad away. There were many other questions to be answered by the transformations study and much scientific groundwork to be accomplished before even beginning. At this point I had no idea that my research would prove that NDE's are a real human perception, one that changes people forever.

2

The Transformations Study

"When we attempt to imagine death, we perceive ourselves as spectators."

—*Sigmund Freud*

Some important words of advice came to mind as I put together the elements of the Transformations study. They were those of Dr. Raymond Moody, the father of near-death studies, who always warned me that if a research project cannot be summarized in one or two sentences, it will probably not have any significant results.

I took his warning to heart by clearly stating the main question to be answered by the project: *Are there transformative effects from the near-death experience that can be documented?* I wanted to prove scientifically what many researchers assumed, that NDEs change the people who have them. I also wanted to know if these changes are sometimes more than just changes in attitude, as in the case of those who have increased psychic powers or greater intelligence.

The Transformations study would require the help of

a wide variety of experts as well as the use of a number of psychological tests which had been used successfully with large populations.

Since many people in the medical community still consider near-death experiences to be a "wacky" topic, I figured it would be best to enlist the help of the most conservative and well-respected thinkers I could find. I sought the help of medical experts who had done near-death research as well as those who had never even thought about the subject. One such adviser was Wren Hudgins, Ph.D., president of the Washington State Psychological Association. His insights were invaluable largely because he had no philosophical axe to grind and no preconceptions on the issues involved. I also consulted with Justine Owens, Ph.D., of the Institute for Personality Studies at the University of Virginia. She and her colleague Ian Stevenson are authorities on near-death experiences as well as experts in the measurement of personality. She helped immensely in determining how I should measure personality change in the people we were to study.

A great amount of help came from advisers Bruce Greyson and Kim Clark, both members of the International Association of Near-Death Studies, or IANDS. This organization is an international support group for people who have these experiences. At IANDS chapters around the world people who have had these experiences can meet others like themselves who are trying to cope with the mysteries of this marvelous (and at times, frightening) experience of light. These two people—Greyson in Connecticut and Clark in Seattle—possess a wealth of information about near deathers, especially regarding their philosophical viewpoints and other aspects that spring from the experience. Psychiatrists like Stuart Twemlow and Glen Gabbard (experts on out-of-body states), and Russell Noyes (who has studied dissociation), contributed help of a different kind by studying the function of the brain and psyche to see if NDEs have a "mechanistic" explanation. Their work led me in some very fruitful directions.

To exemplify the balance I sought among advisers, Vernon Neppe and Joyce Hawkes are good choices. These two people are as opposite as opposites can be.

Neppe was the director of the Division of Neuropsychiatry at the University of Washington. He has impeccable mainstream medical credentials and has written a classic medical textbook on the subject of antiseizure medications. He has also published more than a hundred papers on parapsychological phenomenon in well-respected journals. His fascinating work in the paranormal has always been approached scientifically. He has the sort of dynamic—and yes, skeptical—mind that allows him to examine freely many fields without preconceived notions.

On the other hand, the healer (she cringes at being called a faith healer) is a former biochemist who has published more than fifty articles in scientific journals. She has traveled to Bali and spent several weeks in the mountains, working with native healers and trying to understand why their art of healing is so effective such a large percentage of the time. She is a firsthand witness to the mind's power to heal. She helped us further understand the link between near-death experiences and psychic abilities.

All of these advisers plus a team of interns and student volunteers headed by my research assistant Shannon Greer helped me deal with the large volume of data and anecdotes that came from almost five hundred people who took part in the formal study. Shannon worked full time on this study for almost two years. She traveled to Japan and met with researchers at the University of Tokyo where she spent two months investigating the cross-cultural aspects of NDEs. She provided continuity throughout the project and has probably heard more near-death experiences firsthand than anyone except Raymond Moody, who estimates that he has heard more than ten thousand!

THE LIGHTNING WENT THROUGH ME

Who were the people we studied? And what sorts of questions did we ask them?

I'll answer that last question first by walking you through the file of one patient in the study group. Let's take Patient Number 44 as a typical example.

Her near-death experience happened thirty-two years ago at the age of fifteen. She was on the telephone in her kitchen with a boy from her high school language class when a bolt of lightning hit the telephone lines. Grounding wires had not been attached to the wires so the powerful jolt of electricity passed through the phone line and struck Patient 44 in the head. Here is how she describes the experience:

"The lightning came through the wires seeking ground and went through me. It came through that receiver, into my ear, blew out my eardrum, burned out my hearing nerve, came down my neck, and went out through my shoulder where it left the house through the pipes of a radiator that I was leaning against. My mother says there was an explosion like a cannon that threw me about ten feet across the room. I still had the handle of the telephone clenched in my fist when they found me.

"I didn't know any of this until much later, because I became instantly unconscious. I was suddenly in another dimension. I don't remember going up a tunnel or anything like that. But I was transported into a very peaceful situation, a place that looked like a very white and bright light. In our everyday experience you would have to squint because you couldn't even look at it. But I could look at it in the state I was in and it was very peaceful.

"To describe it in our language is very difficult. It was like being in an airplane over clouds during sunset. But instead the wavy clouds and the red glow were all around me so I could touch it. To try and describe it in language almost makes me feel dumb.

"The feeling that went with it was utter and total peace. I was not an unhappy person as a kid, so it wasn't as though my life wasn't happy and peaceful. But this was a peace I had never really known before nor since.

"I had no body, but I was contained in some kind of essence. If you were there to see me you would see that I was encapsulated by something that looked like a thin gelatin capsule, similar to those cigar-shaped capsules that you put medicine in. I wasn't controlled by this capsule but it held my senses somehow.

"I had sight and smell and hearing and 'me-ness' in it, but I didn't have a body and didn't care that I didn't have one. It just wasn't important at all. It felt so warm and familiar there. It removed all fear of death. I knew it was the next dimension. I didn't want to think about anything in my life. I wasn't worried. I was very happy there.

"Suddenly I felt like I was being pulled down and thrown back into my body. I was angry. I don't think I have ever before felt such a rage! I screamed and screamed in anger and rage because I wanted to go back to that place with the clouds!

"I couldn't hear a think because there was a loud ringing in my ears. But I could feel my dog Sparky licking me the way collies do when they find you and they are frightened. It was about that time that my mother found me. She estimates that it might have been four to six minutes after the lightning struck."

PHILOSOPHY, HISTORY EXAMINED

After telling the story of her experience, we took Patient 44's personal and medical history. By finding out what surgeries, prescription drugs, or psychiatric treatment she had had, we would be able to tell if those experiences had any influence or link to her NDE.

We also took details of her childhood, with an emphasis on possible child abuse or neglect, since some researchers think that people with abuse in their childhood are more likely to have near-death experiences than those who do not. After interviewing more than seventy children and not finding any connection between child abuse and their NDEs, I tend to disagree with this assertion. I still did not want to leave any stone unturned in my research.

The personal history also included spiritual value questions: how much does Patient 44 value spiritual matters over material wealth? What percentage of her income does she give to charity? How many hours a week does she volunteer to needy agencies?

We learned about her spiritual values by asking a series of "Long-Term Effect" questions, like:

- How do you feel about God and religion?
- How do you feel about your own death and death in general?
- What is the meaning of life?
- Summarize your feelings about nature. About suicide.

And so on. There were fifteen such open-ended questions all aimed at finding out the patients' feelings about spiritual matters and the influence the NDE may have had on those feelings.

Although these questions may seem simple ones to answer at first glance, try writing your true feelings about them. Many people break into a sweat when they try or simply can't form opinions about many of these very basic questions. There are a couple I find almost impossible to answer. Yet over 90 percent of the near-death experiencers who replied to our study were able to answer all of these soul-searching questions.

After the personal history questionnaire we gave Patient 44 (and all the other participants in the study) a series of standardized tests. These tests are used by other researchers on a variety of patients, not just those who have had near-death experiences. We used them to compare the results with a large segment of society to see how NDEers stack up to the "normal" population, those who haven't had near-death experiences. I'll briefly summarize the tests so you can see the extent of our examination:

Profile of Adaptation to Life

This four page test is used to score people in such areas as depression, spirituality, drug use, eating habits, and degree of happiness about life in general. PAL is frequently used by therapists to assess a patient's response to therapy and even a job applicant's suitability for a job.

Typical of the questions asked in this test are: In the past month, you have spent time with a friend 1) not once 2) 1–2 times 3) 1–2 times a week 4) daily.

Death Anxiety Scales

We used two. The direct one is the Templer Death Anxiety Scale, which asks a series of fifteen True/False questions such as: "I am very much afraid to die." "I am really scared of having a heart attack." "I often think about how short life really is."

Another of these death anxiety scales was hidden in the Reker-Peacock Life Attitude Survey, a very subtle and clever test for assessing how happy people are with their lives and what is important to them.

Instead of asking yes or no questions, it makes statements and asks the subject to rate how strongly they agree or disagree. For example, Patient 44 was presented the statement: "Life to me is very exciting." She was then asked to rate an answer from strongly disagree to strongly agree. Other statements are: "Some element that I can't quite define is missing from my life." Or, "I feel that I generally make my own choices in my life."

Greyson Values Survey

Developed by noted near-death researcher Bruce Greyson, this questionnaire determines what is important to a person, such things as physical fitness, understanding oneself, prayer, world peace, money and material things, and personal success.

Subjective Paranormal Events Questionnaire

Since one of the most curious claims made by many near-death experiencers is that they develop psychic powers, we included a questionnaire to examine these claims more closely.

This was a hotly debated area by some of the study's advisers who felt that to examine such claims would lay the entire project open to skepticism and ridicule. I felt differently. Although I was skeptical of the claims of increased psychic powers, they came all too frequently to ignore.

I felt that we had to keep an open mind. If we ignored claims of increased psychic powers—or worse, discredited them—we might miss one of the most fascinating transformations of all.

I pointed out to my fellow researchers that I too was skeptical about psychic powers, but that it wouldn't hurt to collect the stories of ESP and precognition for analysis. Besides, we had already accepted as real an experience in which people leave their physical bodies and see beings of light. Why wouldn't psychic experiences like telepathy and dreams of the future be just as likely?

After all, extensive government research over the past twenty years has led to some strong support for the paranormal.

I was not interested in proving or disproving psychic experiences. I wanted to understand who has these experiences and what they mean to them. Specifically I wanted to know if near-death experiences lead to an increased perception of such experiences. Do they act to unlock such hidden potential already within us? Such questions beg to be examined.

This turned out to be the most productive aspect of our study, resulting in a major new understanding of near-death experiences and a wide array of psychic experiences, but I am getting a little ahead of the story.

With the group's blessing I included the Subjective Paranormal Experience Questionnaire (SPEQ) developed by Dr. Neppe. This lengthy profile helps the subject examine his psychic feelings and rate any experience he might have had as being validated or unvalidated. This questionnaire is perfect for skeptical scientists who do not want to take a stand on the objective reality of paranormal experiences, but want to study them anyway.

Validated experiences are ones that have plenty of details or were told to other people before they happened. A person who has never had an NDE has, on the average, less than one verifiable psychic experience in their lifetime. Near-death experiencers, I found, have many times that number. One such example came from Patient 44, who has had three verifiable experiences since her near-death experience more than twenty years ago. Here is one example from her file:

"I was driving to work and I was in a really good mood. Suddenly I became very depressed. I was confused and scared. I was crying and felt the way I would feel if my kids had died.

"I was so scared that when I got to work I called the school to see if my kids were all right. They were so I called a neighbor to see if anything was wrong there. She told me that at 8:10 that morning, just as I was driving to work, my kitten had been run over by a car and killed."

Another verifiable experience comes from one of the patients in the study who suddenly felt a sharp pain in her shoulder while at work. That was followed by a strong sense that someone at home had been hurt. She called home and got her daughter who was crying. The police had just called to say that her husband had rolled his automobile on a country road and broken his shoulder.

Unvalidated experiences are important too. These are characterized by feelings that come true. Feeling that the telephone will ring and it does. Or thinking about someone and getting a letter from that very person the next day. These were important too in understanding the function of the brain and how it remembers. More about that later, too.

The final piece of paperwork for Patient 44 and all the others to fill out was the Temporal Lobe Events Questionnaire. Neppe developed this questionnaire to explore the issue of temporal lobe sensitivity, the area of the brain I believe is associated with increased psychic abilities and near-death experiences.

In previous research I had shown that all the elements of the near-death experience come from the temporal lobe, that area of the brain located just above the ears. In *Closer to the Light* we called this area the seat of the soul because all the elements of the near-death experience except the experience of the mystical light were either generated or passed through this area.

Some skeptics took this discovery to mean that we did not believe in near-death experiences, that by finding the area where they occurred in the brain, we had somehow proven that they were not real. In fact the opposite is true. By finding their location in the brain, we had proven that they *were* real. We had shown that they were tangible experiences and should now be taken seriously by all physicians and not just dismissed as some kind of bad dream.

By discussing my seat of the soul hypothesis with Neppe, we came to realize that virtually all psychic and mystical experiences begin in the temporal lobes. Perhaps having a near-death experience makes more of the temporal lobe available to people, unlocking unused areas of it.

SEEING A FUTURE TRAGEDY

I am reminded of the experience of one person, typical of those who made me more curious about the role of the temporal lobes in paranormal experiences.

Robert Darby is a fifty-four-year-old computer programmer who nearly drowned in a river in the Deep South. He says he never struggled for air when he fell into the water. Rather he felt peaceful and serene.

While underwater he saw a bright light like the sun shining through the water in front of him. For years he thought it was the sun, but the sight of it was so deeply imprinted in his mind that he came to believe it was some other kind of light.

Like so many other NDEers, Robert thought he had seen the sun. But the fact that he felt no fear and felt serene while being bathed in a loving bright light is a certain indication that Robert had a near-death experience. He felt that his NDE had made him psychic about events, but a recent experience had left him puzzled and disturbed. He had a vivid and verifiable dream in which he saw a bus crash that actually happened the next day. Not only that, he personally acted as an escort "up the tunnel to heaven" for those who had died in the accident. As he told it:

"In this dream I floated out of my body and was high in the air as though I was in an airplane. I could see snow on the ground and a yellow, diamond-shaped warning sign. There was an arrow pointing in the direction I was heading and a shaft of light that illuminated the sign. I could see the Rocky Mountains and I remember saying to myself, 'I'm forty miles outside of Denver.'

"Suddenly there was darkness and a violent and jarring crash. I turned to the passenger next to me and comforted her. 'It will be all right,' I said.

"I felt us rising in the air and sensed that we left something dead behind us. There were about six or seven of us and we were in a large, level area. Suddenly a bright orange light appeared above us that glowed brighter and brighter. As we watched it we were filled with joy. It was like being in the mountains on a beautiful day.

"We came to a place where there were many figures, some

of them dressed in robes. One called out, 'You have finally made it.' We were all filled with joy."

Then Robert woke up.

At work, he told of the dream to some of his close colleagues.

At 10:30 A.M. he heard a bulletin on the news that a bus with twenty-two people on board had crashed in the mountains outside of Denver. Six people were killed. Television pictures that night showed that the accident had taken place just past a diamond-shaped caution sign.

This story illustrates the potential value of study instruments like the Temporal Lobe Questionnaire. It is certainly possible that this man's childhood near-death experience triggered a lifelong temporal lobe sensitivity. If such experiences are not collected and examined by standard tools of scientific research, psychic events like these would always be fodder for supermarket tabloids.

HOURS OF SCRUTINY

By the time Patient 44 was finished with the interviews and the questionnaires, she had spent at least four hours under the scrutiny of one of my study assistants or myself. This involved being interviewed in person or on the telephone and filling out a thick packet of information. It was that way with all of the near-death experiencers who agreed to participate in the study. They were not paid to be in the study. Their only compensation was the chance to learn more about themselves and the effect their near-death experience had had on them.

This must have been sufficient remuneration for most of them, because an astounding 53 percent completed the entire study. By the end of the study we had compiled data on more than 150 near-death experiencers. This high completion rate and the large number of people we examined in detail meant we were able to produce valid results.

Many additional hours were then spent by the study staff analyzing each of the patient files. Their main concern was analyzing the material for "internal consistency." This means that we compared their values surveys with such things as dietary habits, charitable habits, and other information from their personal history files. This would help us discover people who were not being truthful with us or who were even lying to themselves.

To test the validity of their stories we had some clever "lie" questions embedded throughout the test. These questions were designed to screen out people who were not telling the truth about their experience or who were greatly embellishing the facts. For example, we asked: "During your near-death experience, were your feet ever cold? If so, was it the right or left foot?" Since we have never heard of a near-death experience that involved cold feet, we expected the answer would be "no" for those who truly had had the experience or who were not making up at least portions of their story.

Very few of the test subjects answered these "lie" questions wrong. For the most part, the people willing to be studied were genuine in every sense of the word.

The people who participated in the study were adults who had near-death experiences as children. I wanted to make sure that the study group had had their near-death experiences in childhood because this group would be less likely to be culturally biased than a study of adults who had NDEs as adults. Children would not necessarily believe that the experience should change their lives. If we used adults who had the experience as adults, there was a strong chance they would expect the experience to make changes in their lives and try to exaggerate what those changes might be.

Another requirement was that at least ten years had to have passed since their experience happened. Any transformations would then have to be considered long-term, not just the temporary kind that last a few days or months after the event.

The time rule—the need to have at least a decade between the near-death experience and participating in the study group—had an important effect on the study. We found that many had lived their lives without ever hearing of near-death experience. Raymond Moody's landmark book *Life After Life* came out only fifteen years ago and only in the past five years has there been such widespread exposure of the subject in the media. As a result, many people who joined the study did not know they had had a near-death experience until we told them. Many state outright that the experience had had little or no effect upon their lives. The results of the study proved how wrong they really were.

This story illustrates the point. I was in my office one afternoon explaining to one of my young patients how a tonsillectomy is done. He was being checked into the hospital the next day and needed reassurance from me that the surgery would come off without a hitch.

His grandfather had brought him to the office and was sitting there as I explained all of the possible side effects. When I finished, he looked up from his reading and said, "When are you going to tell him about the tunnel? That's the scary part, but it was kind of fun, too."

"What tunnel?" I asked.

"You know, the tunnel that curled all the way around like a seashell and turned into light."

I found out later from his medical records that this gentleman had had a tonsillectomy when he was four and had nearly died from an overdose of ether. I convinced him to join the study. Although he denied that the experience had had any effect on his life, his psychological and psychic profile matched many of the others who had been deeply transformed by the experience.

FROM LAWYERS TO LINE WORKERS

Finding near-death experiencers who represent a cross-cut of the population has never been an easy task. In fact, to my knowledge, the only truly objective study of adult near-death experiences is the one done by Atlanta cardiologist Michael Sabom. He systematically interviewed consecutive survivors of heart attacks, asking them to share their experience of being nearly dead.

His patients had two distinct types of near-death experiences. The first type was what he called *autoscopic*, in which the patients claimed to separate from their bodies and float to the ceiling. As a group they were highly accurate in describing their own resuscitations.

Sabom meticulously documents many episodes in which the patients describe readings on machines used to restart their hearts and stabilize their conditions, machines which were not in the patients' line of sight even if their eyes had been open.

The second type of experience Sabom's patients described was called *transcendent*. Often these patients did not have the experience of seeing their own bodies. Rather, they floated away to another realm, one filled with luminous light. Once there they often met heavenly beings which some of them called "God."

Sabom's method of interviewing consecutive survivors of a near-fatal episode is the best way to study near-death experiences. As long as the number of people being interviewed is large enough and the hospital treats people of all races and income levels, you will have a "representative sample" of society.

Some researchers have advertised in supermarket tabloids for their study groups. In such a study, it is difficult to examine medical records or document the authenticity of the experiences. The people found through this method are likely to have told their stories many times, possibly changing details over the years.

Another study method has been to examine only accident victims who did not lose consciousness as a result of their near-fatal trauma to see if they had NDEs. Other researchers have interviewed only patients who did lose consciousness as a result of near-fatal trauma to see what they remembered about being in the never-never land of unconsciousness.

Raymond Moody, founder of near-death studies, simply collected the stories of many different patients in hospitals. He then analyzed the content of their stories and divided them into the common elements of a near-death experience: leaving the body; going up a tunnel; seeing beings of light. It is these symptoms identified by Moody that have remained as the backbone of this research. In many ways, Moody's anecdotal research is the strongest, mainly because it was done before near-death experiences were recognized in mainstream society.

Now nearly everyone has heard of them. Instead of trying to keep them a family secret, people are usually more than willing to talk about them. They do so freely now, which is good. After all, making these experiences a normal part of life is what all of us researchers have wanted all along.

To find a pure study population I drew on many sources, trying to find subjects from every walk of life. We sought out auto mechanics, computer technicians, assembly-line workers, clerks, lawyers, doctors, musicians, television personalities, homemakers, accountants, the list goes on and on. I made sure that all economic groups were represented as well as religions and ethnic backgrounds. We also selected people from across the country, not just one or two geographic areas. We wanted the makeup of our study population to be very similar to that of the American population as a whole.

These patients came to us through referrals from other doctors who knew I had an interest in this subject. When I appeared on radio talk shows, did television programs, or newspaper interviews, I always announced a phone number for people who had had these experiences to call.

One of my favorite methods was to give a lecture on near-death experiences and then, at the end of the talk, explain that I needed people to join the study who would ordinarily be too shy or too busy to volunteer for such a project. Some of the best subjects came from that group.

For example, one woman volunteered after a lecture. She had had a near-death experience as a child, but was very cynical about others who'd had similar experiences, feeling put off by the touchy-feely atmosphere she found at most NDE support group meetings. The only reason she volunteered was that she agreed with me. As she said, "If skeptics like me don't talk, we'll never understand the true nature of the experience."

She proved to be a gold mine of unbiased information. Her experience had been a brief one:

"I was eight years old when I almost drowned in a swimming pool. I remember a deep black void. Then suddenly there was a bright light and I felt a strong sense of peace. I remember talking to the light and struggling to stay in the light. But I was told that things had to be done. Then I came back."

I gave her all the tests discussed earlier in this chapter. She had a very low fear of death—as shown by the two death anxiety tests—and a very strong zest for life. An answer she gave to one of the questions illustrates that: "Every day for me is spectacular. Every day is a sunrise. I love life. It makes perfect sense."

The tests and interview showed that she had more in

common with those touchy-feely weirdos than she thought.

Another hidden gem was a man who challenged my belief that children have pleasant or happy near-death experiences. He said that his childhood NDE just left him feeling bewildered and frightened. As he told it:

"I was fooling around in the water when I fell and hit my head. I floated out of my body. I saw my mother who was in a total panic. She was yelling at my brother and telling him that he killed me when he pushed me in.

"I felt that I had to go back to my body, but I was holding back because I was afraid of getting in trouble for playing where we weren't supposed to. Suddenly I heard a voice say: 'You're going back, we have plans for you.'"

These two examples are typical of the type of people we sought out for this study. Of course, we also wanted the "believers," since they have an important story to tell too. But we needed to examine the nonbelievers and skeptics who had had NDEs and still did not quite believe what they had seen. Even though it was difficult and time-consuming to find these people, it was certainly worth it. After all, the *only* way to discover the true nature of the near-death experience is to examine the full spectrum of experience as it happens to believers and skeptics.

We compared our near-death experiencers with five other groups, all of whom received the same battery of tests and questions:

Adults Who Survived Serious Illnesses as Children but Did Not Describe Any Sort of Near-Death Experience

Comparing this group is important because it is possible that simply surviving a near-fatal illness or injury could give a person the same appreciation for life that is credited strictly to NDEers.

Adults Who Had Vivid Experiences of Warm and Loving Light, Either as Children or Adults

This was a category I didn't know existed until we published *Closer to the Light*. Since then, I have heard from dozens of adults who describe intense and vivid experiences of light. Let me emphasize that these are normal adults who are not near death. Yet they describe this light in the very same mystical terms as those who have had near-death experiences. Here is one example:

"When I was eighteen, my father and I were driving up to my favorite place, my grandfather's cottage. When we went through the gates of the driveway, we realized that the hot summer had changed the cottage and the grounds. There was no life, no birds singing and the grass had all turned brown. The lake was covered with brown algae. I commented to my dad that our little world had died.

"Quite suddenly, the clouds darkened and it began to rain. That was when my father disappeared. The clouds opened and a brilliant light shone down on me. I was bathed totally in loving and feeling light."

The person who had this experience wrote to me asking if this was the same as a near-death experience. Clearly it was not the same, since he was not near death nor even frightened of dying. Yet his experience is not unique. I have talked to many people and received letters from many more about the same such experience. I wanted to compare them to near-deathers to see if they had the benefits of the NDE without having to face death.

I was glad that I included this group, since their presence in this study led to a much greater understanding of spiritual experiences.

Adults Who Identify Themselves as Mystical or Spiritual

Many people claim to have mystical or psychic powers, but few of them have actually been tested. Indeed, few of them have even had definable mystical experiences. Do people who think they are psychic have as many verifiable psychic experiences as NDEers? This would be a golden opportunity to compare these two groups.

I was astounded by what we found.

Finally, Adults Who Had Out-of-Body Experiences as Children

Some researchers think that out-of-body experiences are simply a variation of near-death experiences. The main difference, they say, is that one doesn't have to be near death to have an "Obie."

I felt it was essential to include normal adults who had had out-of-body experiences as children. For one thing, it is the most common paranormal event, with 16 percent of the American population claiming to have left their bodies at least once in their lifetime.

This would be an opportunity to see if OBEs and NDEs were truly the same.

All of these groups would then be compared to a group of "normal" adults, ones who had never had serious illness, mystical experiences of light, out-of-body experiences or, of course, near-death experiences.

The point of all this was to answer one question: *Are there effects from near-death experiences that can be documented?*

Whew!

WHY MY INTEREST?

I have often been asked why I am so interested in near-death studies. Frankly, it is because I believe these stories. These stories are told with such beauty and simplicity by children and adults alike who have nothing to gain by making them up. They demand to be investigated.

I did not always feel this way. When I first heard of near-death experiences, I thought they were just hallucinations generated by medication or lack of oxygen. I, like most of my peers, thought they were some sort of psychological defense mechanism designed to soothe the fear of dying.

After four years of medical school and two years of residency training, I had helped patients cheat death many times. Yet never once did I hear one of them speak about going up a tunnel to another world. Now I realize that many of my patients might have had near-death experiences. I just didn't spend enough time listening to them to find out.

Luckily, a shy and pretty seven-year-old girl told me about a vivid NDE that occurred when she nearly drowned in a community swimming pool and was clinically dead for nineteen minutes.

While casually telling me what it was like to almost die and to come back, she must have noticed the shocked look on my face. "Don't worry, Dr. Morse. You'll see, heaven is fun!"

After that story, my life has never been the same. I realize that there is room for emotion and spirituality in medicine. After researching NDEs all these years, I have heard plenty of both, untainted by a need to please. These stories are straight from the heart.

My co-author describes near-death experiences as "paranormal events that happen to normal people." That fact comes through in the wonder and enthusiasm with which these stories are told. As one NDEer said: "Just when the door closed on my life and everything was black, another door opened and I walked into a new world. Nothing has been the same since." When people say things like that, the stories have a powerful and provocative impact, leading me to think about God and the nature of the universe itself.

Before reporting the results of the Transformations study, let me share some of these marvelous stories:

PATIENT 1: "IT'S NOT HER TIME"

"I got sick when I was nine years old for no reason that I knew of. My fever was about 106 degrees or above. I'd seen the doctor several times and when it became obvious that I wasn't getting any better he decided to put me in the hospital.

That did no good. Over the course of the next few days it went even higher.

"They did every test they could think of but they couldn't find the cause of the fever. Finally a team of three or four pediatricians decided that they had to bring the fever down or I would get brain damage. I was very weak at that point. I heard doctors express their concern that I couldn't stand this fever much longer.

"Finally these doctors decided to take drastic measures. They stripped me naked and wrapped me in ice cubes and a sheet. Then a nurse stood there and took my temperature every few minutes.

"When I got all wrapped up I passed out. I seemed like I was floating and everything around me was dark and pleasant. And then there it was, a tunnel of light with a very bright light at the end.

"I was being helped by someone to move up this tunnel. When I arrived at the end there was a lovely vista spread out before me. There were all fields with flowers and there was a nice road over on my right and the trees were painted white halfway up and there was a white fence. It was lovely.

"And there were the most gorgeous horses I had ever seen in the pasture off to the right. I would have to cross two fences to get to these horses but since I was nine years old there was no doubt where I was going.

"I started off that way and after a little while there was a white kind of light, a presence beside me that was friendly and not at all threatening. The presence said: 'Where are you going?' And I said: 'I'm going over there.' And he said: 'That's great. We'll come along.'

"There were a lot of flowers that I had never seen before

and I was asking him their names and picking them as we went along.

"And I was talking to this blinding white light that was all colors and no colors at the same time. And it didn't have a face or features per se, but that didn't bother me. I remembered looking back down the tunnel at the people crowded around the bed and I didn't care that I was up here and my body was down there. I felt very good, as a matter of fact.

"So I was talking to this light and wandering over to these horses. I had just gotten my leg over the top rail of the fence and into the horse pasture when this voice out of nowhere said: 'What is she doing here?' And the light answered: 'She came to have the horses.' And the voice said: 'It's not right. It's not her time. She has to go back.'

"At this point I was clutching the rail because I didn't want to go back. That was the *last* thing I wanted to do. And the voice talked to the white light a little bit more and they decided that I would have to go back. So I threw a tantrum. I pitched a royal fit. I grabbed on to the rail of the fence and wrapped my arms and legs around it and I wouldn't let go. The voice just laughed. 'Look, you can have it later, but this is not the time. And throwing a tantrum is not going to do you any good.'

"I found myself floating over the field and going back down into the tunnel. And I was screaming and yelling and kicking and biting and everything else, and this hand was just gently guiding me down the tunnel that I had come up. 'Why can't I stay?' I yelled. 'Because we have something for you to do,' said the voice. I felt this hand gently guiding me back down this tunnel I had come up and I popped back into my body.

"I remember lying in my bed looking up. A frightened doctor was standing next to my bed. He sighed with relief and said to one of the nurses, 'Oh good, she's back.'"

PATIENT 2: "I WAS WRAPPED IN A WARM LIGHT"

"My experience happened to me between the sixth and seventh grade. It was during the summer and I was up at the lake where we had been waterskiing all weekend. I was skiing with another guy, double skiing. I fell forward and the rope wrapped around my arm. The rope kind of 'zipped' and cut all the way through my skin and muscle, all the way to the bone. I was in intense pain and then I passed out. Later I went into shock from loss of blood and the pain of the experience.

"Anyway, the driver of the boat didn't know I was still attached so he kept it on full power. For about thirty seconds he dragged me behind the boat and I was pulled underwater.

"I remember thinking that I was a goner. Then I remember thinking that I didn't care. The pain went away and although there was a rush of water going by me, I couldn't feel it.

"I was wrapped in a warm light. I didn't go up a tunnel like I have heard of people doing, but I did separate from my physical body and I was able to see myself briefly, speeding along underwater, bleeding from my arm, without a care in the world.

"My life flashed in front of my eyes and I specifically remember thinking just how cool my life had been. I thought of my accomplishments so far and all the fun I'd had and was glad to have been here. I knew I was going to die at this point and was willing to accept my life for what it was. Oddly enough it was the most peaceful feeling I have ever had.

"Finally the fellow driving the boat figured something was wrong and he shut the throttle down. I came to the surface at that point because I was wearing a life preserver. It was sheer panic at that point. I came back into reality and was in intense pain. They rushed me to the hospital and began treatment. I was in shock for about eight hours and the doctors said I almost died from loss of blood."

PATIENT 3: "I SAW LIGHT GOING THROUGH THIS TUNNEL"

"When I was about nine years old my sister and I were at the beach. She was baby-sitting me and she took me down to a rocky beach where the waves would crash onto the shore. We went way out, picking up shells and not paying much attention to what was going on around us.

"Suddenly I was hit by a big wave and I was washed between rocks and dumped into some deep water. I remember swallowing tons of water that seemed to fill my lungs. I remember being terrified as I just dropped to the murky bottom of this pool.

"All I could feel was bubbles and bubbles, but I couldn't breathe at all. I saw light going through this tunnel and then I was in the most beautiful garden I had ever seen.

"My short life went in front of me and then I was in front of a big figure, a light that I think was God.

"It was so beautiful that I didn't want to leave. But he knew what I was thinking and he said that I had to go back.

"The next thing I remember is someone pulling my head up. I had been carried over to the bathhouse and was lying there when I woke up. The lifeguard had pumped a lot of water out of my lungs and he thought I should have been dead. I was lucky in a lot of ways that day."

PATIENT 4: "I COULD SEE MYSELF"

"I was four and my sister was eight and she was afraid to go down in the basement to get a toy so she sent me. The light didn't work down there so I took a flashlight.

"I started down the steps but decided to point the flashlight up at the burned-out bulb to see what a light that was burned-out looked like. That was when I fell off the side of the steps and landed on the cement floor.

"I don't remember falling. The next thing I remember was being up by the ceiling, looking down at myself. It was not totally dark in there, so I could see myself lying facedown and not moving.

"I just watched there and waited for me to do something. But I didn't do anything. I didn't breathe and I didn't move. I just hovered up there thinking that I must be dead.

"I was very relaxed and I felt good. I just kind of waited to see what would happen. Then I realized it was getting lighter in the cellar. It was actually getting lighter and lighter and the light was coming from behind me. I looked behind me and there wasn't any wall, just this small and very bright light way up high. It kept getting bigger and bigger. It was just a light but it was the most beautiful thing I had ever seen.

"Just as I was turning to go toward it my mother came through the door. She rushed down the stairs and found me looking gray and not breathing. She picked me up and shook me and that started me breathing again. Then she took me up to her room and called the doctor.

"That is all there really was to the experience except that it was the most remarkable thing that has ever happened to me, and the most wonderful."

PATIENT 5: "LOOKING DOWN A PEEPHOLE"

"I was sitting in my fifth- or sixth-grade classroom when I got sick and everything started to go dark. I managed to get up to the teacher and ask if I could go home. I don't remember much after that but the teacher said that she had two girls walk me home. I was very sick and had an infection in my leg that later put me in the hospital.

"I guess I was lying on my grandmother's sofa when all of a sudden I was looking down a peephole. I could see another place through that peephole. There was a stone path and lots of greenery and I remember seeing a trellis and a stone wall.

"There was a beautiful woman in a long dress who was smiling and holding out her arms. I saw a young girl going toward her that I think was me. I could feel love and happiness as I observed the whole scene. The woman seemed to swoop down and pick the girl up and they twirled around, laughing and hugging. The feeling was incredible and the whole picture was beautiful.

"After I got well, I referred to this experience a lot. When things got bad in school or at home I would talk about my 'tunnel vision weird thing.' I didn't know what else to call it."

PATIENT 6: "I FELT COMFORTABLE AND VERY GLAD"

"When I was sixteen I had a near-death experience while undergoing surgery. It was very intense and personal and one that I have shared with few people over the years.

"I had been given anesthetic and was totally out, sleeping the kind of sleep that you are supposed to when undergoing surgery.

"All of a sudden I was traveling somewhere and then I was

with a Being that radiated unmeasurable love. I felt comfortable and very glad to be with him. I thought about my young life and all the physical problems I'd had and said: 'I'm glad to be done with that one.' He didn't agree. 'You didn't do much,' he said patiently.

"Immediately I was filled with a sense of having a mission that was left undone. I said: 'Oh you're right, maybe I should go back.' And like that I was back in my body, full of pain. I felt so heavy and restricted inside a body. I was full of anger. I said 'maybe' I should go back. I didn't say I wanted to go back.

"I calmed down quickly. Since then I have always had a sense of a mission unfulfilled. I feel I am supposed to be doing something for mankind. I became a nurse but have not gotten over that feeling that I have yet to discover exactly what it is I am supposed to do."

AMAZING RESULTS

The results of the Transformations study were exciting. After we finished analyzing the data from the more than four hundred people who participated in the research project we discovered that the near-death experience causes many long-term changes in the people to whom it happens. These changes include:

A Decreased Death Anxiety

Near-death experiencers have approximately half the fear of dying that the normal population does. When asked for their feelings about death, the typical NDEer would say something like: "I no longer fear it," or "I now know that we go to a better place when we die."

This very common written response corresponded with their low test scores on the death anxiety questionnaires.

An Increase in Psychic Abilities

Those tested in the NDE group had more than four times the number of validated psychic experiences as the normal and seriously ill group. Not only that, but they had twice the number of verifiable psychic experiences as those we tested who claim to be psychic.

Many of us wish we could tell the future, but this is rarely good news for the NDEers who suddenly discover that they have the power to do just that, as you will see from chapter four on this subject.

A Higher Zest for Living

NDEers have the positive traits of the type-A personality, which means they have a drive to work hard without negative compulsions like anger and the willingness to step on others in their march to the top.

Many describe themselves as workaholics who are constantly busy because they "can't get enough of life." Once again I point out that these people have the positive traits of those who work hard and are labeling themselves incorrectly when they call themselves workaholics. Zestaholics would be a more appropriate name, since they exhibit such energy and enthusiasm about life.

I had to laugh at one NDEer's description of herself: "I'm not like most people who have these experiences. I'm busy all the time, working in my garden and thinking about living. I'm not spacey like most of those people." I had to explain to her that most of "those" people aren't spacey. They are living zestfully just like her, not dwelling in the ether as some people think.

A Higher Intelligence

Although this is difficult to prove, it is almost impossible to ignore. Many of those in the NDE group felt they had evolved into higher beings, becoming more intelligent as a result of their brush with death and the spiritual experience it caused.

Is it possible that the experience itself leads to increased intelligence? Or is it that the experience leads one on a different approach to solving perplexing problems?

I believe that increased intelligence really happens to some NDEers, although I cannot say why. I decided to examine the stories and people in detail to see if there was any concrete reason for increased intelligence. What I found stunned me.

The rest of this book is devoted to the results of the Transformations study and the stories of the remarkable people who participated in it.

We have kept the text largely free of statistical analysis, to keep the writing clear of scientific jargon. Realizing how important it is that you be able to see our scientific data, we have included it in the appendix on page 239.

I also want to note here that some of the stories you will be reading are from people who were not a part of the Transformations study. Some are from people who contacted me to discuss their experiences after reading our first book, *Closer to the Light*. Although they were not a part of the study, their experiences are used, sometimes to illustrate important points from the study and sometimes because they are just good stories.

But wait, Dr. Morse. Do you believe in life after death? I am asked this question at every lecture I give.

I answer with a Buddhist joke that goes like this:

A student asks a renowned holy man if there is life after death.

"Why ask me?" replies the holy man.

The student is stunned by this reply. "You are a spiritual master who speaks with God!"

"That is true," says the holy man. "I am a spiritual master—but not a dead one!"

3

Not Afraid to Live—or Die

"Only three things are certain: death, taxes, and fear of both of them."

—*Woody Allen*

About six months before the Transformations study was completed I was on a late night talk show suffering through an interview with a particularly rude and obnoxious radio host. He asked me to define the real significance of the near-death experience. I answered that it was a genuine spiritual experience and should no longer be dismissed as a hallucination by medical doctors.

"These people are having a spiritual experience, not something that can be explained away as just a bad reaction to medicine," I said. "The significance is that it's a real experience and doctors shouldn't downplay it because we can't explain it."

"So what's the big deal, Doc?" He growled. "So what that they have these visions when they almost die?"

I stammered a response: "If more medical doctors

would allow a spiritual side to exist, then the near-death experience could make our hospitals and intensive care units more user friendly."

The talk show host growled again. "So what's the matter, Doc? Afraid patients are going to start suing you for missing out on their near-death experience?"

It was a minor confrontation that left me at a loss for words. After examining the results of the Transformations study, I can answer that "so what" quite easily. We can learn some very important lessons about approaching life—and death—from near-death experiencers. If we are willing to put aside our growls of skepticism and that need for all-knowing scientific approval, we will find a group of people whose experiences have made them so much less fearful of death that they have become true connoisseurs of life.

Proof is in the Transformations study, where we found that the people who had NDEs, especially those who experienced the warm and loving light, were ignited with a zest for living that was coupled with virtually no fear of death.

As Dr. Stuart Twemlow told a reporter from *Life* magazine, "People who have near-death experiences may never fear death again. Their faith is strengthened so that the sense of catastrophe with which they live is finally mastered. The NDE has a healing effect."

This is best seen by analyzing the information we gathered on death anxiety. We used two methods of scoring death anxiety. One was the Templer Death Anxiety Scale, which is a fifteen-question test that measures fears and obsessions. The other test is named after its creators, Reker and Peacock.

It consists of several questions designed to be hidden in other test questions so the test subjects won't even know they are being asked about their fear of death. By scattering these questions throughout the tests, we prevent the test subjects from hiding their true feelings about death.

We also compared death anxiety to the experience of light by using the Greyson Near-Death Experience Validity Scale. This scale was developed by Dr. Bruce Greyson as a way of validating the experience and measuring its depth.

We discovered that adults who have had near-death experiences as children have a much lower fear of death than people who have not had them. This was true whether they had vivid and wonderful memories of a flower-filled heaven or a brief and fleeting experience of light.

Furthermore, the deeper their experience, the less they were afraid of death.

This finding is in sharp contrast to people who have come close to death and survived, but were not fortunate enough to have had a near-death experience. They actually had a slightly higher death anxiety than normal. And New Agers, people who identify themselves as being intensely spiritual, have the same death anxiety as the general population.

Decreased death anxiety does not come from nearly dying or from believing that NDEs are the gateway to an afterlife. It comes from actually seeing that light at the end of the tunnel.

EXPERIENCED SURVIVORS

These results brought to mind the thoughts of Socrates, who pointed out that we have a fear of death, and yet we do not even know what death is. Why are NDEers not afraid of death? As our study group revealed, they have experienced death and survived. They believe that the process of death is not to be feared. They are emphatic on that point. Here is some of what they have to say on the subject:

"It's not death, it's another kind of life."

"Heaven is a nice place to go."

"Death? Not worried about it at all."

"I think about it and it kind of scares me. I do smoke and drink too much. Yet I know the reality of death, and it is nothing to be afraid of."

"I don't fear it. It will be like going into another dimension. Death is simply an open door. I don't mourn too much when people die."

"Death is something that our society fears, and that people learn to fear. It is too bad, because it actually is really nice."

"Well, when it's time it's time. It wasn't too bad the first time."

* * *

These are the words of ordinary people who have one thing in common: as children they actually did die and have never forgotten the experience. They come from all walks of life: housewives, insurance salesmen, laborers, carpenters, medical doctors, lawyers, television newscasters. Across the board they have no fear of death, simply because they have been there and know what to expect.

They want to live. They are emphatic about it. They all feel that their lives have a purpose, that they are here to fulfill a goal. This goal or purpose bestowed upon life by the NDE isn't always filled with an exotic message. Most of the time, the goal is quite ordinary.

For instance, a fifty-seven-year-old owner of a construction firm had an NDE in which the Light told him to "go back, you have a job to do." When I asked him what that job was, he became somewhat angry:

"What do you mean? I just told you that I have my own company and employ seven workers. I have a family and have raised up three children. What more job is there than that?"

Also, they are not suicidal. When asked about suicide, they will typically answer as this person did: "Suicide violates everything that I believe about the values and importance of human life. I can't condemn someone else's decision, but I know that it's not for me."

This sentiment is backed up by scientific data which shows that those who attempt suicide and have a near-death experience rarely attempt it again. In one such study, people who survived jumps from the Golden Gate Bridge were questioned by researchers about what they remembered from the jump. Those who had NDEs did not attempt suicide again. But more than 25 percent of those who did not have NDEs did try to kill themselves again.

OTHER PARANORMAL EXPERIENCES

As part of the Transformations study, we examined the ways other paranormal experiences affect the so-called "zest for life index." We studied out-of-body experiences most closely. Out-of-body experiences are the most common paranormal experience known. As previously stated, some studies have them happening to as many as 16 percent of the population.

The most common out-of-body experiences are simple and brief. A man who is out jogging suddenly sees the top of his head, for instance. Or a woman gets up in the middle of the night to get a drink of water. When she arrives at the sink and reaches for the glass, her hand passes through it.

We gave a large number of people who had had these experiences the same battery of psychological tests that we gave the NDEers. We tested them for anxiety and hostility, aggression and psychosomatic complaints like headaches and stomach pains. Our goal was to see if paranormal experiences that were not connected to NDEs had as profound an effect upon the zest for life index as the NDE.

There were some fascinating out-of-body experiences. For instance, an eighty-one-year-old former newspaper reporter told of his experience thirty-five years earlier. As he tells it, it was late at night and he was dozing by the switchboard. Suddenly he heard a voice say "go" and he floated out of his body and out of the building. He crossed an open field and drifted over the river like a balloon. Below him, snagged on some brush, was a body.

He suddenly zoomed back into his body and awoke with a start. He called the fire department with a "tip" that a body could be found in the river. They found a body just where he told them to look.

Another out-of-body experience came from a thirty-five-year-old nurse in Washington, D.C. Hers was quick and simple; she was lying in bed when she suddenly felt herself float to the ceiling. She could see her body below but felt no fear or discomfort from her new perspective. Finally she just returned.

I expected the out-of-body subjects we examined to be as transformed as the NDEers. These people report many of the same characteristics as the near-death experience, including lack of fear, vivid and clear thoughts, a sense of boundary, and a decision to return to their body.

Yet when we examined the results of their tests, we found that the out-of-body experience was not transformative. This was true even though the experience scored high on the Greyson Validity Scale, meaning it was very similar to an NDE. One of my assistants jokingly referred to the out-of-body experience as a dry run, an experience similar to using a flight simulator rather than actually flying a jet aircraft.

These results lead me to believe that the transformative part of the near-death experience, the portion that leads to positive changes in personality, is somehow contained in the light. When one little girl said that "all the good things are in that light," she may have revealed the greatest truth about near-death experiences.

CHANGED BY THE LIGHT?

The white light is one aspect of the near-death experience that I believe cannot be physiologically located in the brain. As you will read in chapter four, most of the other elements have been found to come from the right temporal lobe. In my own research I have called this area just above the right ear the circuit board of mysticism. It is there that out-of-body experiences are thought to originate as well as some of the other traits of the NDE, such as life review, seeing departed loved ones, and traveling down a tunnel.

The experience of light has no known origin in the brain. That is right. Numerous scientific researchers have documented that every element of the NDE—the out-of-body experience, traveling up the tunnel, seeing dead relatives, having a life review, seeing visions of heaven—can be found to reside in the right temporal lobe.

The only element that cannot be found in the brain is the experience of light. None of the reductionist researchers have yet been able to find the origin of the light in the brain.

By analyzing the data in our study, I found that those who have experiences of light are the ones who have the greatest transformation. And the deeper that experience of light, the greater the transformation. It doesn't matter who has the experience—Marines, punk rockers, real-estate agents, corporate executives, housewives, ministers, or holy men—they are all transformed by their exposure to the light.

The knowledge that something more pleasant than extinction awaits at the moment of death has brought about unique and positive transformations in these ordinary people.

I have no doubt that much of this transformation is due to a reduction in death anxiety, which Ernest Becker, the Pulitzer Prize–winning author of *The Denial of Death* calls, "the basic fear that influences all others, a fear from which no one is immune, the worm at the core of man's pretensions to happiness."

The near-death experience has at the very least reduced this fear to a mere discomfort.

What follows are several case studies, which first deal with the NDE and then the level of transformation.

"A FEELING OF THE MOST COMPLETE COMFORT"

Spencer Christian is the weatherman on "Good Morning America," a network television program watched by millions every day.

I met Spencer in 1990 when I was on that program talking about the research that led to *Closer to the Light*. After the program, he took me aside and told me about his own near-death experience at the age of five. I found it to be a deep near-death experience that led to many changes in his life. I'll discuss those changes after Spencer tells about his childhood NDE.

"I had a near-death experience when I was five years old. I was living in Newport News, Virginia, and I had gone into the hospital for what was thought to be a routine tonsillectomy.

"They knocked me out with ether. While I was in surgery I began to hemorrhage severely and lost a great deal of blood. I know this because I was told, not because I really recall the loss of blood. I was told later that my loss of blood became so severe and I became so weak that I was near dying. The doctors thought they were going to lose me on the operating table.

"However, my memory of what happened while I was on the table is that I regained consciousness while the surgery was going on. I remember seeing the doctors and nurses working furiously over me and I could feel the pulling and tugging of things in my throat.

"The next thing I remember is the sensation of being outside my body and being able to see from some point above the operating table. I was up in a position near the ceiling, looking down.

"I recall feeling a complete loss of fear and panic. I just had a feeling of the most complete comfort and security that I have ever felt. I guess I liken it to the feeling of your mother holding you in her arms and rocking you.

"I don't recall actually encountering a being that I would define as God. But I do recall the sense of having an option as to whether I wanted to go back or not. Somehow I do recall choosing to go back and reenter my body."

Spencer had difficulty describing the experience to his mother, who spent much of the next week by his bedside in the hospital. She believed that her son was talking about a dream, but Spencer always insisted that it was more. It was vivid immediately after and it remained that way for years. "Into my teenage years, I could remember exactly what I had experienced while on that operating table," said Spencer.

During his teenage years, he discovered a name for his experience. He also realized he had one of the major traits of NDEers, low anxiety about death. As he explains it, "It somehow gave me a sense of life being something that continues after physical death."

Spencer shares the positive view of life that most NDEers have. He thinks of life as a "passage . . . a transition into another realm." He thinks this passage has to be a natural one, not by suicide. "I guess if there is a crime against nature, it's suicide. I do believe that life is God-given and I think it's a shame for someone to force that life to end before it plays itself out."

Spencer, like the others transformed by this experience, sees his life as being rich with purpose. "I feel it is the purpose of my life to pass on as much positiveness as I can every day of my life with every person I meet." The intriguing thing about Spencer and others transformed by these experiences is that they can actually articulate a purpose for their life. Most people simply cannot do that.

Spencer, like many other NDEers in the study, feels that part of our purpose in life is to do something that "serves the entire community of mankind." As he puts it: "Part of our purpose in life is to be charitable and sensitive to other points of view and other people's needs and to be open to different perspectives and tolerant of different cultures."

Although Spencer has been extremely successful in his career, material possessions are not high on his list of needs. He rarely lends his name to highly commercial ventures. Rather he sponsors a series of videotapes that help people with the practical aspects of death and dying. These tapes are nuts and bolts advice on how to make a will and deal with life-support issues. Family and education are important to Mr. Christian. "Education is important beyond my ability to define its importance," he says. "Family and friends are probably more important to me than anything else I can think of. I think I derive my sense of self-esteem and my positive feelings and my sense of being at peace with the world from a very caring, loving family."

"THERE IS PEACE IN KNOWING"

Almost thirty-five years ago at the age of ten, Jan was on vacation with her family on the rocky coast of Maine. Her twelve-year-old sister was baby-sitting her. The two girls became bored with staying at their cottage, so they decided to take a walk down by the beach. While jumping from one rock to the other, Jan slipped and landed facedown in a deep tide-pool. She immediately inhaled water and remembers to this day the panicky feeling of "trying to use her lungs as gills." Then something unexpected happened.

"The very first thing that happened is my life flashed before me. I could see scenes from school and family dinners, nothing very important, just flashes.

"Then I went through a tunnel or something like it that wasn't very long. There was a beautiful light on the other side, so beautiful that I didn't want to leave. All around me was a garden where the plants were all bright.

"In the light I could see a figure that I know was God. I wanted to stay with him but I didn't. Someone pulled me out of the water and pumped my lungs."

When Jan awoke she was undergoing chest compression to clear her lungs of water. Her parents took her to the hospital where she was examined by a doctor and released the same day.

Her NDE lasted probably a few seconds. But the results have continued on until this day. For instance her death anxiety is three, less than half the level of that experienced by the normal group. When asked why, she simply shrugs and says: "There is peace in knowing. I've seen the life beyond and it's peaceful."

Wherever she was during the NDE, Jan wanted to stay there. Now she is glad to have returned. "I was given a purpose for my life in the light," says Jan.

She is a mother with three kids who works full time in a bakery. In her spare time (and I don't know how she could possibly have any), she works in a hospice where she helps cancer patients ease the pain and fear of dying.

"I tell people about my experience and how it changed me," she says. "I tell them that I saw heaven when I died. It seems to help."

"BE A GOOD MOTHER"

Suzanne, a fifty-three-year-old mother of two, had a near-death experience twenty years ago. She was not included in the Transformations study because she did not have an NDE in childhood. I am including her in this chapter because hers is an example of an NDE that led to an immediate and very visible transformation.

For nearly fifteen years Suzanne was married to an abusive husband. To the outside world, her husband seemed like the perfect man. In the privacy of their home, Suzanne suffered through almost daily sessions of slapping and shouting. She wanted to divorce him, but her religious parents told her to stay married and maybe things would change.

After fourteen years of miserable marriage, Suzanne experienced what she now calls "a stroke of luck." While reaching into the glove compartment of her car, she failed to notice that the traffic ahead had come to a stop. She slammed into the rear of a stopped car while going approximately thirty-five miles an hour.

She was taken to the hospital with internal bleeding. While her injuries were being assessed she had a cardiac arrest.

"In the midst of all this hospital chaos, I just zoomed out of my body and into a tunnel. I was walking down a tunnel with the most beautiful light at the end that was enveloping and warm.

"I could feel myself being surrounded by the most loving arms and my cheek could feel the warmth of a being against whose chest I seemed to be leaning. There were people in the distance and I wanted to go greet them.

"A man's voice, very warm and caring, held me back from going to the people. The voice seemed to be coming from whoever or whatever was holding me in that wonderful loving warmth. The voice said, 'Suzanne, turn around.' I turned around and I saw my children standing in midair. Then the voice said: 'Go back and be a good mother.' "

Suzanne's life changed dramatically and immediately as result of that message. She left her abusive husband and stopped going to the church where he was a mainstay. She went back to school and struggled as late-in-life students do to get a degree. After a few years, she remarried and now has the marriage and home that she wished she'd had all along.

Her faith is still intact, although in a different form. "I don't go to church anymore, but I have a deep personal faith. For the longest time I thought that the warm entity that held me was Jesus and I was sure that the experience was a testimony to my faith. But I can never be a part of organized religion again. After standing so close to the light, I can't bear bureaucracy in religion anymore."

"I WAS DRAWN TO THIS WHITE LIGHT"

Darla is a forty-five-year-old housewife in Arizona whose brush with death came when she was having her tonsils taken out at the age of six.

Her family lived in a rural area of the Midwest so there was no convenient hospital in which she could have this relatively simple surgery performed. Instead, she went to the doctor's office where she was put to sleep on an examining table by a doctor using ether. The doctor used too much of the anesthetic and Darla had a cardiac arrest.

Here is the experience as she tells it:

"There was a dark period but I had the sense of moving through something. This must have been going through the tunnel.

"Then I came out. I say 'came out' because it seemed as though I came out the other side. When I came out I was drawn to this white light and I remember thinking, 'This is so peaceful. This is what heaven is.' It was just this incredible feeling. Like metal being drawn to a magnet, I was being drawn to the light.

"There was no face in the light like some people describe. I didn't see God or anything. It was more like energy and it was very wonderful.

"Then I began to think that I really wanted to stay there. I really didn't want to go back. Then I thought about my sisters. I was the oldest of four girls and it came to me that their lives would be ruined if I didn't go back.

"I had a strange thought, too. I thought that my father would kill the doctor if I didn't come back.

"From somewhere I was able to see everyone down below. I was able to see the doctor shaking me and the nurse who looked extremely scared. Their faces were so vivid to me that for years I could have picked them out of a crowd.

"When I came back to life I knew I had been to heaven. Things were very different for me from then on. I was much more easygoing than my sisters. They would get bothered by things like whether they had a date or not but those things never really bothered me.

"I think the difference in me was caused by the way I now saw time. It was very different after that experience. I realized that time as we see it on the clock isn't how time really is. What we think of as a long time is really only a fraction of a second. Thinking like that really made me less materialistic."

THE LIGHT "TOOK ALL OF MY FEARS"

At the age of fifty-one, Dana thinks she wears her NDE in her smile. She is a well-adjusted person who is very aggressive in her approach to life. She was married at twenty and has started and owned a number of businesses, including three beauty shops and a commercial artist studio. As her top five priorities in life she places children at the top of the list and helping the sisters in her Catholic church. Her fear of dying is almost nil, according to her test scores.

Her attitude all stems from the near-death experience she had more than forty years ago. As she tells it:

"When I was eight or nine, I was sick with measles. There were no antibiotics in those days and my illness became critical.

"My parents were taking turns sleeping with me to keep an eye on me. On this particular night, I remember feeling just terrible and waking up. But I wasn't in my body, I was hovering above it, looking down on my mother and I.

"My mother was awake and she noticed that I wasn't breathing. She called for my dad who ran into the room and began shaking me.

"I went up a tunnel at this point. I was headed for a light but at the same time there was a voice in my head that said, 'Let her go back. She isn't ready yet.' I went into this beautiful bright light anyway. It was a beautiful feeling that totally took all my fears of death away.

"Then I came back."

All of the people here—indeed all of the people in the Transformations study—have experienced the same changes as a result of their NDEs. They have a zest for living that outstrips all those around them. They are virtually fearless about death. *And* for that matter, virtually fearless about life. They live very firmly "in the now," savoring life as it happens, making as much of it as they can.

They are literally transformed in such a way that they aren't afraid to live or die.

LEARNING FROM OTHER EXPERIENCES

So what? say the skeptics. *So what if near-death experiencers don't have a fear of death like the rest of us? So what if they are zestful about life? So what if they are less likely to have deep depressions and feelings of futility that lead to suicide? So what? What does that have to do with the rest of us?*

The answer is simple: Learn what you can about life from these brushes with death, even if they are the experiences of other people.

That is what Barbara did. She has never had a near-death experience. Yet by living through her sister's fourteen-year battle with leukemia, one that included a deep NDE during surgery, she gained many of the insights and traits of the average NDEer. In short, she learned about life from someone else's near-death experience. Here is her story:

"My sister and I were very close. We always told each other everything, as so many sisters do. She was several years older than me and in many ways she functioned as my teacher.

"Her long journey with leukemia ended in 1980. For almost fourteen years she was in and out of the hospitals and had to endure probing, poking, and surgeries while going through recurring bouts and remissions.

"It was during some kind of surgery for one of these battles that she almost died. She was quiet after that for some time. But one evening while we were sitting in our bedroom together, she told me of her experience. I could tell by the look on her face that this was a unique and sincere thing that had happened.

" 'I was on the table,' she said. 'All of a sudden I could feel myself being pulled upward. It was slow at first, then the pace became increasingly faster and faster. By this time I was in a black tunnel, but at the end of the tunnel was a light. As I got closer to it, it got brighter and brighter. It wasn't like any light I could describe to you. It was beautiful.

" 'When I was almost to the end, I slowed down and then I was there. This light was so bright and it surrounded me and filled me with a total love and joy. I don't know how else to describe it to you. I felt intensely pure, calm and reassured. I just wanted to stay there forever.

" 'The next thing I knew, my life was flashing in front of my eyes, everything that I had ever done in my life. After that, I felt myself falling back down the tunnel, faster and faster until I was back in my body.'

"She said that the experience left her unafraid of her disease. She believed that the light was Jesus and that she had been given a chance to see the heavenly light.

"After that, there were many changes in her life. She became the one with the courage. Before facing a medical procedure or after receiving a dire medical prognosis, she was the one who put everyone at ease. She still suffered, but she seemed to have a different attitude as though she knew that the end wasn't really the end."

When her sister died in 1980, Barbara realized that she herself had become a different person. She missed her sister greatly but found inspiration in the way she lived out her last days. Rather than lose faith and become depressed as many people do at the loss of a loved one, she found new appreciation in the gift of life. "What my sister saw in another world has made my world a much brighter place," she says.

BETTER ABLE TO COPE

I have heard many stories like the one above, people who were healed and even transformed by the near-death experiences of others.

Here is another one from a seventy-one-year-old woman in Michigan:

"Oddly enough, I have been able to cope with the death of my husband of forty-four years as the result of my niece's deathbed vision.

"She died at the age of ten after having cancer. She was so ill that she could not lift her head from the bed. Yet just hours before she died, she suddenly sat up in bed and told her mother: 'You can't go with me! The light is coming to get me but you can't go! I wish you could see it. It's so beautiful!'

"Shortly after that, she died."

Of course, the family was distressed by the loss of the niece, but all of them felt comforted by the little girl's vision of light. They didn't say "so what?" or dismiss it as a hallucination. They believed—as did the girl—that she had seen her next destination and would soon be finished with this suffering.

A few months later, the woman's husband died unexpectedly of a heart attack. Although she was grief-stricken, her grief was tempered by the memory of what her niece had seen: a beautiful light with good things in it.

So what? you might ask. Well, for one thing this woman now has a better chance of escaping what is known as the widow syndrome, in which a woman dies shortly after the death of her husband. Some researchers speculate that such a death can be caused by the immune system's being depressed by grief. A widow who can accept the death of her husband is more likely to have a positive emotional state, a strong indicator of adjustment to grief.

Both of these women mentioned above illustrate the value of NDEs even to the people who didn't have them. Both were transformed by someone else's experience. Just hearing the dying person's belief that they are not facing extinction is comforting information to loved ones.

A paramedic at Children's Hospital in Seattle, Washington, told me just how important this information can be in comforting frightened or bereaved relatives. He told me that he often discusses my research with the families of the critically ill people he deals with on an emergency basis. He tells a family that he will do everything he can, as quickly and efficiently as possible. He explains that my research has revealed that patients are often conscious during the process of dying and often think they are in control. He tells them people who have survived these resuscitations report that it is not agonizing or painful and that it is often harder to watch the resuscitation of a loved one than it is for the person himself. He goes on to say that many people find being near death a mystical experience. Some see a bright light that they call God. They may even see long-dead relatives and be given a chance to stay where they are or return to earth.

"If they die, it probably won't be a fearful experience for them," he says. "But one thing is for sure. If they live they will approach life with a new zeal and gusto that you aren't accustomed to."

MEANING FOR ALL

So what does having a near-death experience mean? For the people who have had one the answer is easy: they have seen the light. Regardless of who they are or what they do, our research shows that NDEers cannot help being transformed by their experience.

I had the opportunity to see this firsthand when I went with several of my teenage patients to "The Oprah Winfrey Show" in New York. They fell upon each other like brothers and sisters, excited to meet so many others who had had this experience of light.

These kids knew each other instantly, yet from surface appearance they seemed to have little in common. Katie is a devout Mormon who is a cheerleader at her high school in Idaho. Mark runs a health club in Los Angeles and is very physically fit. Violet is a New Age punk rocker whose wild hair and black clothes made the Oprah producers cringe. Skip is a nerdy-looking genius who entered college at the age of sixteen.

All of them looked very different. Yet on the inside they were very much the same. They had been called crazy, had been told that their experience wasn't real. Sometimes they had even been called liars. Yet they knew the experience was real because it had changed their lives. I can vouch for that, because all of them were a part of the Transformations study and had a very high zest for life index. And now they were all together with no need to explain themselves. As one of the kids said to me, "We all belong to the same club."

So what does it mean to those of us who have not had NDEs? I will answer that with a true case study that reads like a parable. This is the experience of a man who had a very deep NDE:

"I was in a garden. All the colors were intense. The grass was a deep vibrant green, flowers were radiant reds, yellows, and blues, and birds of all beauty fluttered in the bushes. Everything was lit by a shadowless brilliance that was all-pervading.

"This light did not cast a shadow, which I realized when I cupped my hands tightly together and the palm side was just as light as the back side. There were no sounds of motors or discord or commotions. No sound but the songs of birds and the sounds (yes, 'sounds') of flowers blooming.

"Behind me through a glasslike wall were throngs of people going through their daily business amid commotion, noise, shouting, dirt, grime—people with problems—people as we see them every day.

"In the garden room above me I became aware of voices—singing voices—yet in the garden there was only one person visible.

"I went over to him to see what he was doing. He told me that he had a large stack of messages and that he was attempting to send them to the people that I could see through the glass wall.

" 'They have problems,' he said. 'And I have messages that I would like to give them that will help them. But they won't stop worrying about their problems long enough to look this way and let my message come through to them.' "

Near-death experiences and our reactions to them have far more to tell us about our culture's relationship to death than they do about the existence of an afterlife. We have ignored death and hidden it away in hospitals, where patients die in the cold company of medical machines. The fear of death has become all-pervasive in our lives, and undermines our own happiness. Near-death experiences are appealing in part because they redeem the ghoulish mess we have made of dying. To many, NDEs provide some of what religion has previously provided, a way to talk about death before it comes, and a glimpse of death as a passage rather than a termination. The near-death experience tells us that we all have an inner voice that, if only we would listen to it, would tell us that death is not to be feared, and that life is to be lived to the fullest.

4

Seeing with the Mind

"The truth is sort of mysterious and sometimes has nothing to do with facts."

—*Oliver Sacks*

For more than a decade I have studied near-death experiences. Virtually all of the people who have them, regardless of background, report psychic experiences as a result of their NDEs. That means simply that housewives, lawyers, secretaries, journalists, musicians, doctors—the entire NDE population—report psychic experiences ranging from precognition to telepathy.

Most of the time, these psychic experiences are simple and insignificant. For instance, many people have premonitions of telephone calls. They tell a co-worker or member of their family that a specific person is about to call and in a few minutes that person does. Usually it happens with close family members, but often the calls come from people they haven't heard from in years. Since they told other people before the event happened, the experiences were verifiable psychic experiences.

Some people are able to predict the death or serious injury of a person with great accuracy.

Still I had what I call a medical-school bias toward psychic experiences. For that reason it made me uncomfortable to hear patient after patient describe psychic experiences with authentic and verifiable details.

For example, one woman who had a near-death experience during World War II while her father was overseas told me of an unusual dream that came true.

She dreamed that her father was on a boat and that she sensed danger for him. In her dream, she reached out with her mind and bumped the boat to safety.

The next day they received news that her father's ship had almost been destroyed by a mine. A long line of ships were in line at a dock. As her father's ship began to pull forward, it suddenly stopped, shaking as though it had run aground. Another ship took its place in line and hit a floating mine.

After listening to so many cases like this one, I became more comfortable with paranormal experiences. I realized that either all of these people were making these stories up or their NDEs were truly giving them some kind of psychic powers.

I also realized that I had been approaching this issue in the wrong fashion. My medical-school bias against psychical abilities simply is not based in science, but rather my own ignorance of the science that has examined the paranormal. I discovered that there is a wealth of scientific information on a great variety of paranormal abilities that firmly backs up the existence of extra-sensory abilities.

I owed it to the courage of my subjects to push aside my irrational skepticism and treat their experiences with the respect they deserved. I decided to take my own advice and at least listen to the experiences.

In the Transformations study I set out to document these paranormal experiences. I wanted to know if NDEers have more psychic experiences than people who have not had them. I wanted to know if these experiences could be verified. Were other people told of them before the experience occurred? Is there something unique about the NDE that unlocks hidden potentials within the human brain? We found that NDEers do indeed have more psychic abilities than the normal population. And we are not talking about a slight increase in abilities here. People who have had near-death experiences are four times more likely to have psychic experiences than those who have not had them.

I want to point out that we only documented the experiences these people had and whether or not they could be verified. We didn't try to demonstrate the psychic abilities of NDEers by having them read minds or try to guess which card was on the top of the deck.

Previous psychical researchers have focused primarily on proving the existence of paranormal *abilities*. I applaud their valiant efforts, some of which have been quite successful. Not only have there been scattered case reports of psychic powers, particularly telepathy, but some psychic powers have been reproduced in a laboratory setting. For example, researchers at the Dream Laboratory at Maimonides Medical Center in

New York have yielded statistically significant results in many of their telepathy experiments. Some of these experiments have a person looking at a postcard of a classic painting in one room while a study subject sleeps in another room. When the study subject shows signs of REM sleep (the point in sleep when dreams occur) he is awakened by researchers who ask what he is dreaming.

A very high percentage of the time, the study subject is having a dream that greatly resembles the painting being examined in the next room.

Still these results are not widely accepted by the scientific or medical community. Perhaps the problem is that we do not know enough about these experiences to study them adequately. For instance, before the concept of electromagnetic fields was understood, it was impossible even to conceive that such fields existed around the world. The only evidence people in the Middle Ages had of electricity was lightning and the magician's rod which was charged with static electricity and discharged a visible spark to the delight of the awestruck audience.

The irony of science is that the scientific method sometimes destroys our ability to study a phenomenon. As scientists have known for some time, the simple act of observing an experiment can actually change the outcome of that experiment. That means there is a huge difference between saying "something doesn't exist" and saying, "I cannot document in a reproducible fashion that something exists."

THE MINI-GELLERS

An excellent example of this comes from a story I heard at an international conference. It was told by a researcher who conducted a study of several "mini-Gellers," ten- to twelve-year-old boys who claimed to be able to duplicate the spoon- and fork-bending abilities of famed psychic Uri Geller. Although many of Geller's bendings were exposed as frauds, some were not. This researcher found that Geller's performances inspired some of these boys to be able to do the same thing.

The researcher studied several of them. He suspended a piece of metal in a sealed bottle and gave the boys one week to bend it with their minds. None of them were able to bend the metal in the set time, although they claimed to be able to stop and start watches and bend spoons away from the observation required in a study.

Certainly this study could be taken to disprove such claims of psychic power. Yet there is more to this story than numbers and statistics indicate. One of the boys *insisted* that he could bend a kitchen fork. He showed the researcher a fork that he had bent at home and it did seem to be bent in an unusual fashion, with no marks or other signs that a tool was used.

As the week progressed, the boy became obsessed with bending the metal in the bottle. The researcher and his co-researcher were caught up in the boy's enthusiasm and measured the metal twice a day with special instruments that could detect the slightest bend.

A week went by and the metal didn't bend. They informed the boy that the experiment was over and dismissed him.

Late that night, the researcher was called by his co-researcher. There, still enclosed in the sealed bottle, was the piece of metal, bent in an odd fashion.

Did the boy coil the metal? Was it the researchers who—in their encouragement of the boy—did the bending? Was it a combination of all three? Did the boy finally relax and therefore tap some force in his mind? The researchers had verified that the human mind can bend metal. But they didn't understand the mechanism well enough to reproduce it in the laboratory. And worst of all, since the bending didn't occur in the proper setting and time frame, it didn't count scientifically.

Since psychic experiences are so difficult to reproduce in a laboratory setting, I merely set our sights on verifying the authenticity of the people who had these experiences.

As I have already mentioned, the findings were remarkable. We found that NDEers have four times as many verifiable psychic experiences as people who have not had NDEs. Many of these we jokingly referred to as ordinary psychic experiences, meaning that people foretold future events that were not very exciting. For example, one woman seemed to know when someone was going to spill a glass of water or have a minor accident. She was frustrated and angry at not having any way to prevent these accidents, especially since she had frequent foreknowledge of them. Some of the experiences were quite extraordinary, as you can see from the following examples:

"I WAS OVERCOME WITH THIS TERRIBLE FEELING"

One of the people in the Transformations study had been "blessed" with psychic abilities since having his near-death experience at the age of five. Most of his experiences were of the ordinary variety. For instance, he had a dream while he was in high school that a girl came running into one of his classes with the exciting personal news that her boyfriend was coming home from college to visit. Two days later, a girl ran into his chemistry class shouting the disrupting news that her boyfriend was coming home from college for a visit.

Other times he was able to predict telephone calls, surprise visitors, and other ordinary events like that. In 1980, he sensed an incident that gave him full confidence in his hunches. He tells the story:

"I was living in northern New Jersey but working about forty-five minutes away from home near New York City. It was late afternoon and I was sitting in this little neighborhood restaurant and bar having a sandwich with a couple of buddies of mine.

"We were sitting there having a normal conversation and eating a sandwich and soda when all of a sudden I was overcome with this terrible feeling that something had happened to one of my kids. I don't know why but it was a very strange feeling and I had never sensed anything like that before.

"I was in a panic. I said to my friend, 'I've got to call home. I've got this strange feeling that something's wrong. I've got to call home.'

"He said, 'Okay, yeah, go ahead,' and was obviously frightened by the look in my face.

"I went to the phone and found out that at virtually the same moment that the feeling overcame me, my son had been riding down our street on a neighbor's bike and the brakes failed. He continued from our street through an intersection, a very busy cross street where there always is a tremendous amount of traffic at that time of day.

"Somehow he had zoomed through the intersection untouched by the traffic and ended up in a ditch across the street.

"My wife was looking out the living room window of the house and saw the whole thing. She couldn't believe that he wasn't killed by the traffic. She sounded very frightened on the phone and said it had just happened minutes before I called."

"I DREAMED MY UNCLE'S DEATH"

Another example of enhanced psychic abilities comes from a woman I shall call Sandy. She tried to kill herself when she was twelve years old. She was having trouble with her family and was shuffled from one relative to the next for almost a year. Finally she decided she had had enough. She gathered all the prescription medicine she could find at her aunt's house where she was living and sat at the kitchen table with a pitcher of water and began swallowing pills as quickly as she could.

After about a half hour, she passed out. Instead of blackness, she saw a bright light. "It wasn't like natural light or electric light," she said. "It was like nothing I had ever seen."

A Christ-like figure appeared to her and spoke without moving his lips: "Why are you doing this? How could you give back the greatest gift I have given you? You should go back and find a place where you will feel more comfortable so you can learn more about me."

In the meantime her aunt had discovered her and called the fire department. Sandy awoke to the taste of ipecac being poured into her mouth by a fireman to make her vomit.

A good deal has changed for Sandy as a result of her NDE. One of those changes has been in her ability to see the future.

"On a regular basis, I dream what will happen the next day. I'll often witness conversations in my dreams that actually take place the next day, or I'll dream events that happen the next day. For instance, I dreamed that I was going to meet a guy on the street and we would spend the entire day together. The very next day that happened. This kind of experience has happened to me over a hundred times, I'm sure.

"I didn't used to believe these were real until I dreamed my uncle's death. He was in perfect health but on this night I dreamed that he was going to die suddenly. The next day he died of a heart attack. When my parents told me I just said, 'I knew it was going to happen.' Since then I've always believed my dreams."

"I WAS SHOCKED ACROSS THE COUNTRY"

This psychic event occurred while the person was having his near-death experience. It happened about fifty years ago during World War II, to a man we shall call

Ted. He was working in Texas at a plant that made projectiles for navy cannons. His girlfriend had moved to San Diego, California, with her family about six months before he nearly died. He had never been there.

One day he was greasing an overhead crane at this plant when he touched some electrical wires. He was "frozen solid" by the current, unable to move.

It was almost a minute before someone on the ground realized he was being electrocuted and cut the power. In that short period of time, Ted had an experience that could certainly qualify as psychic.

"I was sitting up there being shocked and the next thing I knew, I was in a strange place. I was in the air, going across a playing field. There was somebody with me but I couldn't see who they were because I couldn't turn my head.

"All of a sudden as we crossed this field, there was my girlfriend. She was walking along with her books to her bosom, arms clutched in front of her, heading toward this little house in a housing development outside of San Diego.

"I had no idea where it was, but I could see two things: I could see a baseball diamond backstop and I could see a water tower with writing on it.

"I was with her as she walked. I could see the back of the houses she was headed for and knew which one was hers even though I had never been there."

A few months later, Ted quit his job and took a bus to see his girlfriend. When they got to the fringe of San Diego, Ted suddenly had an urge to get off the bus. He told the driver to stop and got off "out in the boondocks."

"This was a long time ago, and San Diego was just a puff of a town. I got off and started to walk in the direction of the bus stop. I looked up and saw the water tower I had seen when I left my body! I looked over and saw the baseball backstop in the playing field that I had passed over! I saw the backs of a row of houses and walked up to the one I had seen in my experience. It was the right one."

Later Ted did some calculations. His electrocution took place at 2:30 Texas time, which was 12:30 California time. His girlfriend was going to summer school and she walked home after class every day at 12:30, crossing that playing field.

"I was shocked across the country," Ted says of his experience. "And to this day it gives me goose bumps to talk about it."

"I SAW THEM TRY TO KILL MY BROTHER"

One of the most fascinating psychic experiences of all in the Transformations study is from a woman I shall call Anne. She nearly died as a young woman from an adverse reaction to medication. She went into a type of shock that closed her windpipe and virtually choked her to death. Before doctors could help her, Anne's heart had stopped. While they worked to restore her heartbeat, Anne had a full-blown near-death experience.

After the NDE, Anne began to experience periods of precognition in which she knew things were going to happen before they did. This happened to her dozens of times. When a neighbor's dog was run over she knew it was going to happen because she had dreamed it the night before. When someone was going to break a dish at the dinner table or in the kitchen, she somehow knew it and was oftentimes caught flinching well before the shattering started. One time she had a feeling that a person had been hurt in a car accident across town. She told other people about it and later the premonition turned out to be true.

These experiences disturbed her family. None bothered them as much as the time she announced that someone was going to try to kill her brother, who lived across town. Anne saw it in a dream that she told her family about at the breakfast table the morning after she had it. She saw her brother coming to her out of the dark, screaming in pain. He had blood dripping from both hands and an open wound in his belly. He was screaming.

The dream was very disturbing for her. She told her stunned family. On account of the location of the wounds, it was suggested that perhaps she had dreamed of Christ and the crucifixion. Anne insisted she had dreamed of her brother's future.

Two weeks later, her nightmare came true. Burglars broke into her brother's house. He confronted them with a gun and shooting broke out. As he came around the corner of a room holding his weapon in a two-handed grip, one of the burglars fired a shot that passed through both of his hands. A shot also struck him in the abdomen. They left him bleeding on the living room floor and screaming in pain.

"I saw them try to kill my brother," said Anne, who found the psychic experiences too much to bear. She went to a neurologist who prescribed medication to make her sleep very deeply and to quell her temporal lobe seizures. She has taken this medication for nearly four years to drug the psychic abilities right out of her. Anne says she would rather have the groggy feeling of being constantly medicated than the recurring psychic experiences.

THE BABY "TOLD ME THAT HIS ARM HURT"

This fascinating story was told to my co-author by the man who had it, an immigrant from Soviet Georgia we will call Yuri. Although he was not a part of the Transformations study, I think it's important to include him since he illustrates the wide variety of psychic experience which can happen to NDEers.

One night while waiting at a bus stop in his home country, Yuri was hit by a car that careened out of control and jumped the curb. The bystanders at the scene thought he had been killed instantly and Yuri himself had a strong sense of being dead when the ambulance came to take him to the morgue.

The statement "having a sense of being dead" is somewhat contradictory. Yet it is one of the symptoms of a near-death experience. I can only imagine that it is somewhat like being consciously aware of your dreams or consciously aware of things going on around you as you sleep.

Anyway, Yuri was consciously aware of being dead and of being taken to the morgue. He knew that he was lying on a cold metal table and also that he was considered dead by the doctor who examined him.

Since he was a dissident, Yuri was put in cold storage

until an autopsy could be performed by a doctor from Moscow. Apparently that was the way officials in the state of Georgia could protect themselves from charges that he was assassinated. Yuri was locked in a cold storage cabinet for three days before the doctor from Moscow arrived only to find that he wasn't dead.

He was aware of much that happened while he was in that cold cabinet. He knew that he was "dead." And he knew where he was—locked in a morgue waiting to be autopsied.

At some point during the three days, Yuri saw a "pinhole of light." He began crawling toward that tiny speck of light and realized that it was very far away. Still he kept crawling until he reached the speck of light. There was a small opening but the light drew him because of its intensity. He began to squeeze through the tiny hole and suddenly he slipped through to the other side and into the light!

At that point he found himself surrounded by a light so brilliant that it "burned my eyes like fire." He tried to find the pinhole that would let him crawl back into the darkness but it wasn't there anymore. Gradually he adapted to the light and found that it gave him certain freedoms.

For one thing, Yuri could go visit his family. He saw his grieving wife and their two sons, both too small to understand that their father had been killed.

Then he visited his next-door neighbor. They had a new child, born a couple of days before Yuri's "death." Yuri could tell that they were upset by what happened to him. But they were especially distressed by the fact that their child would not stop crying.

No matter what they did he continued to cry. When he slept it was short and fitful and then he would awaken, crying again. They had taken him back to the doctors but they were stumped. All the usual things such as colic were ruled out and they sent them home hoping the baby would eventually settle down.

While there in this disembodied state, Yuri discovered something: "I could talk to the baby. It was amazing. I could not talk to the parents—my friends—but I could talk to their little boy who had just been born. I asked him what was wrong. No words were exchanged, but I asked him maybe through telepathy what was wrong. He told me that his arm hurt. And when he told me that, I was able to see that the bone was twisted and broken."

The baby had a greenstick fracture, a break in the bone in his arm probably caused by having been twisted during childbirth. Now Yuri and the baby knew what was wrong, but neither had the ability to communicate the problem to the parents.

Eventually the doctor from Moscow came to perform the autopsy on Yuri. When they moved his body from the cabinet to a gurney, his eyes flickered. The doctor became suspicious and examined his eyes. When they responded to light, he was immediately wheeled to emergency surgery and saved.

Yuri told his family about being "dead." No one believed him until he began to provide details about what he saw during his travels out of body. Then they became less skeptical. His diagnosis on the baby next door did the trick. He told of visiting them that night and of their concern over their new child. He then told them that he had talked to the baby and discovered that he had a greenstick fracture of his arm. The parents took the child to a doctor and he x-rayed the arm only to discover that Yuri's very long-distance diagnosis was right.

These anecdotes represent the wide variety of psychic experiences NDEers have had: telepathy, precognitive feelings, precognitive dreams, seeing other people and places through some kind of remote viewing, being able to diagnose illnesses and sometimes even acting as healers.

After examining the data on paranormal experiences from the Transformations study, I agreed with the great psychologist William James, who pointed out that any theory of the soul or mind that ignores altered realities and paranormal experiences cannot hope to be complete.

What does it mean that so many NDEers have these paranormal experiences? It might mean that these "paranormal" experiences are really quite normal. I think it also means that the full resources of the human mind have yet to be tapped and the near-death experience activates that part of the brain that has our dormant psychic abilities. After all, when so many healthy, normal adults describe dreams that come true, visions of the future, and other such "paranormal" events, maybe they aren't paranormal.

Maybe they are just unique.

Psychic experience often appeared during the Transformations study. And these experiences happened to NDEers and those around them. Here is an example:

A woman in the study named Katherine told me a wonderful tale that made me question the very nature of everything around us.

Her mother was dying. She had had a stroke as a result of complications from diabetes and was on a very serious downhill slide. She could not speak and was unconscious.

Katherine spent considerable time with her mother during her last days. She described her mother's final hours as being "very intense," like someone clinging to the edge of a cliff.

That evening Katherine went home and about ten o'clock she fell asleep with one of her daughters.

Early in the morning "something" woke her up. The room was filled with the overwhelming smell of lavender, which is one of the hallmarks of psychical experience, according to the parapsychological literature. She looked at the foot of the bed, and saw a little girl with long brown hair tied by a ribbon, holding a rag doll.

"She looked at me with pure energy," Katherine told me. "She seemed to be drifting toward my daughter, which frightened me. 'Don't go near my child,' I thought. Then the little girl disappeared."

A few days later, when her mother died, Katherine returned to her parent's home. Among her mother's possessions she found a large container of lavender scent. Also in an old trunk was a picture of her mother as a little girl, looking the same as the girl Katherine had seen at the foot of her bed. Katherine had not seen the picture before, nor had her mother used lavender scent.

Katherine is a forty-year-old businesswoman who has been married for fifteen years and has two children. She has a good family life, enjoys her job and appears to be normal in every way. Yet this experience can only be described as paranormal. Somehow she shared her mother's death experience.

Throughout the Transformations study, people report predeath visions and shared death visions as common examples of psychic experiences. I have been contacted by many people who are not a part of the study who claim to have had predeath visions. Some have even told me about experiences in which they feel they should contact a person, only to find out later that the person was having a near-death experience at that very moment. A woman named Jane in San Diego told me about one such experience.

While being raised in the South she had a close boy-friend named Bill. At about the age of eighteen, she joined the Navy and moved away. Bill married and the two went their separate ways.

Jane hadn't seen or heard from Bill in more than thirty years. Then one day, while working in her garden, she had an unexplainable urge to call him. She contacted old friends and discovered that he still lived in the same town they grew up in. She got his number a few days later and found out from his daughter that he had been in the hospital with a massive heart attack. About a week later she spoke to him.

By comparing notes, they realized that he had just been taken to the emergency room when she first had the notion to call. He told Jane that he felt his spirit leave his body. He could see the doctors working on him and his daughters in the waiting room, frightened for his life.

He had a life review and saw Jane as she was thirty years ago. It was one of the high points of the review, he told her. He had never felt such a deep sense of peace, love, and contentment as during that experience. "But when they asked if I wanted to stay in the Light or return, I decided to return and take care of my private matters."

He told Jane that "pretty soon I am going to die." Then he thanked her for calling and said: "Isn't it funny that you decided to call me on the day that I was having this happen to me? I haven't thought of you in years."

STRANGELY COMMON

It is strange. But does that mean it's uncommon? I think experiences like these are much more common than many think. After examining so many cases of predeath and shared visions, I can only speculate that the same conditions that trigger a near-death experience also trigger the ability to communicate with others. I don't know how such telepathy might work, but I do know that the evidence in favor of it is now overwhelming. Even psychiatrist Sigmund Freud stated that telepathy is a primitive form of communication made dormant by language. By studying the brain mechanisms that are linked to the near-death experience, we may learn precisely how it works.

Take this story, for instance:

Edna and Tom, an elderly couple in Phoenix, Arizona, received the bad news that their daughter had breast cancer. She lived in Milwaukee and the couple immediately flew back to take care of their grandchildren while she had surgery.

The surgery proved to be unsuccessful and the cancer began its slow and steady spread throughout her body.

Edna and Tom had returned to Phoenix by this time but they were constantly on the telephone with their daughter in the Midwest. She had lost a lot of weight and become weaker because of chemotherapy and the ravages of the disease. Still she remained extremely optimistic. She was going into the hospital for another round of chemo and had great hopes that her disease would now turn around.

The night after their daughter's chemotherapy, Tom woke up to see his daughter standing at the foot of his bed. She was dressed in white and glowing brightly. She sat at the foot of the bed and talked to her father. He couldn't understand anything she said but he felt a deep sense of peace at seeing her so "dressed up."

Tom immediately awoke Edna. He was wide awake and talking fast about what he had just seen. Edna didn't question whether it was a dream. Both of them knew what it meant. Their daughter had died.

In a few hours they received a call from their distraught son-in-law telling them what they already knew.

This experience proved to be a very comforting one for the family. No one had expected the daughter to die so quickly and with such little notice. Yet the fact that she had been able to appear to her father at the point of death was great comfort to her family. Even the grandkids were told what grandpa saw. Instead of treating this event as though it didn't happen or concealing it like a wicked secret, the grandparents freely discussed what had happened. It helped pull this family together instead of tear it apart as the death of a loved one often does.

Rather than view life as a senseless chain of events, it made them feel as though their mother had died as a part of a grand plan.

Time and again I have heard people praise the predeath and shared visions as being proof that life is preplanned by God. As one who believes in free will, I have trouble with the concept that we are living a grand plan. But I have no problem seeing how these experiences impart meaning and empowerment to those grappling with death.

PREDICTED HIS DEATH

One such story comes to me from a woman I shall call Linda. Her son was accidentally shot and killed at a party. One of the kids at the party found a gun. No one was sure if it was real or not. They were passing it around when one of the kids took it outside and fired it into the air. "I think it's a cap gun," she said, handing it barrel-first to the boy. At that point the gun went off and the bullet hit him in the chest.

"It's real! It's real!" he shouted before falling dead.

Needless to say the death of her child was devastating to Linda. But the predeath vision her son had two months before his death and another incident have given Linda the hope that her child's death was not senseless. As she puts it: "His death has taught many people about life."

Two months before his death, Linda's son came to the breakfast table looking tired. When she asked what was wrong, he said that he'd had a very vivid dream. He said that a tall lady dressed in white "like a glowing princess" had come to him and told him that time was running short. All the doors around him in this dream closed, and the only place left to go was down a long hallway.

"And that was it," he said. "It was weird."

Throughout the month he continued to dream this same dream. He also drew pictures of things that appeared to him during these dreams. A tall monument was one object. Another was a tree that he drew, with leaves and without.

He did not know what the drawings meant but he continued to produce them and ask his parents for their opinion. Linda wrote about them in her journal and even collected some of the drawings.

Two days before he was shot, the boy went for a walk with his mother. He took her hand and said in the most serious of tones: "If I die, don't cry about it. I know I'm going to be happy there because they showed me. It's beautiful."

Linda was shocked. She asked him pointedly if he was thinking of committing suicide, which he denied. "I just don't think I'm going to be here much longer."

Two days later he was shot in the chest.

On the night her son was shot, Linda awoke with a backache. She sat up and began to cry. She said her upper back hurt and she was afraid something awful had happened. When the phone rang a few minutes later, Linda stood up and screamed "my son is dead," before her husband picked up the receiver and heard the bad news from the police.

When they buried the boy a few days later, both Linda and her husband noticed something they had seen on his drawing pads. The tall monument from a neighboring grave was the same as in his pictures. The same could be said about the tree at the gravesite.

"I have told my doctor what happened but he just discounts it as being an experience caused by a stressful situation," she says. "But I wrote down that he thought he was going to die two months before he died. And I felt the bullet when he felt the bullet and knew it killed him before the police called. I quit talking to doctors about it because they just say I was in shock. But this isn't shock."

This astonishing and heart-wrenching story illustrates how precognition can bring comfort to a family devastated by the loss of a child. Most parents in this situation would be in very bad shape. Death by accident tends to be particularly hard on parents, as it certainly was on these parents. Yet her son's predeath vision holds out the promise that her child's death is not senseless, but instead is a part of some kind of universal tapestry.

It is amazing that an accidental death could be foretold by visions. In the case of dying cancer patients it is reasonable to assume that there is a subliminal intuition about impending death. However, in the case of a seemingly random event like an accidental shooting, how would it be possible to know in advance, unless it was somehow a preordained event? As I have already said, this is a difficult concept for me to grasp since I believe in free will.

Yet I still have many other stories involving predeath and shared visions that I can't explain away. Other researchers such as Phyllis Atwater have documented the same thing. I find these a validation of the paranormal experiences that happen to normal people. They may well originate in the right temporal lobe, that circuit board of mysticism, but that doesn't mean they do not reflect the truth.

BEYOND DENIAL

Some people are afraid to acknowledge until later that their visions could be true. Or, as one woman said, "I thought people would call me a New Ager if I talked about my mother's predeath vision."

What many people don't realize is that denial of such experiences is the newer phenomenon. Our ancestors were well aware of the signs of death, including predeath visions. According to Phillip Aries, the renowned French historian of Western culture, there was no particular difference between the supernatural signs of impending death and the medical signs. Medieval man expected to see heavenly lights and talk to dead relatives as his vital signs failed.

When the philosopher Pascal said that "each man must die alone," he was referring to the irony of a dying person being surrounded by a crowd which was typical of deathbed scenes in the 1600s. Today his words have

lost their irony and instead become simple fact. Most
people die alone, out of control and drugged. But if they
do experience the supernatural aspects of dying, they
often ignore them because they are afraid to acknowledge what their senses tell them.

VALUE OF VISION

Although the nature of the near-death experience has
been studied exhaustively, virtually no studies exist on
the value of predeath visions and other paranormal
events. We do not know how common they are nor do
we have a good idea how families react to them.

Based on my experiences with them, predeath visions
contribute greatly to the healing process of those trying
to overcome grief. I have been told by many people that
the predeath vision of a dying loved one helped them
get over the loss. But do predeath visions occur to a
large number of people who are dying? And are they always helpful for the living?

I think the answer to both of those questions is yes.
But there are few structured medical studies to prove
my intuition. There are only the dozens of stories I have
heard from people who call or write to me because I am
a sympathetic ear in the medical community. People
like the woman in Chicago who said her father awoke
from a coma and said that he had been touching the
brilliant white robe of a being of light and that he was
no longer afraid to die. "It was the fabric of eternity,"
he said. "It was beautiful." Or another woman, who told
me that about half an hour after her teenage daughter

died, the young girl opened her eyes, smiled a peaceful and intense smile at her mother, and then passed on.

These fragments of experience are easily overlooked by hurried doctors who tell hopeful family members that they are just "hallucinations," or "death reflexes." Yet the fact is that they don't know what they are because medical science has done very little research on predeath visions and the value of paranormal events in general.

Maybe it is because studies like these have not been embraced by the medical community or that they are dismissed or devalued by doctors. I am sorry that such an attitude has developed.

As doctors and nurses or family and friends, we need to be in a position to hear these experiences. When those uncomfortable times come, we need to spend time with the very sick and listen to them.

In case after case, I have heard the seeds of healing and comfort for the living come from the visions and premonitions of the dying. The key is to listen. By listening to the dying themselves, we can learn to understand many mysteries of life and death.

I myself sometimes feel torn about how to use this material. For example, a woman in Texas called to ask me a very painful question. Her daughter had sustained a head injury and was in a coma. Ever since the child's accident, the mother had been having dreams of her daughter being stuck in the tunnel that people pass through during the death experience. Could this happen? Could it possibly be that her daughter couldn't continue her final voyage?

I didn't have an answer for that woman, but I spoke

to her for a long time and soothed her fears. Answers don't always come easily, but I can say that being willing to hear and accept a patient's paranormal experiences is an essential part of the bedside manner of a physician who works with critically ill patients.

5

Believing the Unseen

"Patients who confabulate relate the best story that they are able to construct from the data available to them and think it true."

—*William Calvin, M.D.*

The story which I am about to relate seems like a typical near-death experience until the end, when the account becomes puzzling. I am using this example to address the critics of near-death experiences who think that they are "made up" stories.

I borrowed this case study from Dr. Raymond Moody:

A forty-five-year-old grammar school teacher who is married to a prominent Midwestern banker and has two children had an interesting story to tell about the day she died.

She was rushed to the hospital with intense pains in her side. Some tests revealed that the bile duct from her liver was completely blocked by gallstones. To keep her gallbladder from rupturing she would have to have emergency surgery.

She was prepared for surgery and wheeled into the operating room within two hours of the time that she walked into the hospital. Toward the end of the operation she "died." Medical records show that her heart stopped beating and she had no blood pressure.

During that period, something came to life. As she tells it:

"What I remember is this. Suddenly I was awake and I felt so relaxed and happy I thought surgery was over. As I looked around I found that I was rising above the operating table. As I went up, I passed right through my doctor's face, and he had this look of fright on his face. There was sweat all over his forehead.

"I saw that the nurses were pale and people were saying that I was dead. I felt fine. I looked down and I could see my own body on the table with that big gash in my side all sewn up. I wasn't concerned about the body at all. I felt so free. For a moment I felt great concern for my husband and children. I wondered what they would do without me. As soon as I thought that, I immediately stopped, as I knew that the Lord would take care of them. Just then, I saw more doctors and nurses rush in with equipment. They brought in a heart shocking machine and another doctor came in and tried shocking my heart. The surgeon had already given me up for dead.

"Anyway, I then entered into a dark round tube or hole. I could call it a tunnel. I seemed to go headfirst through this thing and suddenly I was in a place filled up with love, and a beautiful bright white light. The place seemed holy. Plants and flowers, I could see beautiful scenes.

"As I walked through this meadow I saw people separated in little bunches. They waved to me, and came over and talked to me. One was my father who had died about two years before. He looked radiant. He looked happier than I had ever seen him before, and much younger. My grandmothers and grandfathers were there too. Everyone was happy to see me. But my father told me that it was not my time and I would be going back. I was disappointed but also relieved that I would be returning to my husband and children.

"Just as I turned to go, as I felt myself being drawn back, I caught sight of Elvis. He was in this place of an intense bright light. He just came over to me, and took my hand, and said: 'Hi Bev, do you remember me?' "

NOT FOLKTALES

This event had many of the core elements of a near-death experience, but did seeing Elvis make it a confabulation or fantasy of the unconscious mind? Was this well-respected woman telling an untruth about what happened when she "died"? Did she make up a story of what she thought should happen based upon seeing me on Oprah or Donahue? Or did she fill in some kind of visual gap in the near-death experience by throwing in an image of Elvis, whom she had shaken hands with as a child?

These questions and others like them confront the most basic question of our research: Are near-death experiences real? Or are they fabricated by patients who watch TV talk shows and read supermarket tabloids and think that this is what they are supposed to see when they die? In short, are these modern folktales?

This is a controversy that has raged in the research community for years. Are near-death experiences simply products of our subconscious fear of death coupled with too many blaring supermarket headlines?

This important issue of cultural contamination is very difficult to analyze objectively. The fact that virtually all civilizations and human beings throughout time have believed in life after death may mean nothing more than the simple fact that all human beings have a deep need to believe that they will live forever. As mythologist Joseph Campbell stated many times, we have lost the myths and heroes which bind us together and help protect us from the unknown. Some researchers have suggested that near-death experiences are our new cultural myths, which help soothe our fears of death, yet have no real basis in reality.

Carol Zaleski, the Harvard theologian, describes the near-death experience as a product of religious imagination. For Zaleski, the near-death experience is simply another sort of religious vision, the kind of experience that hundreds of years ago might qualify someone for sainthood.

In late 1990, Ian Stevenson, the most prestigious parapsychological researcher in the world, published an article in *Lancet* stating that one does not need to be near death to have a near-death experience. He proposed abandoning the use of the name "near-death experience" and recommended instead "fear-death experience" as a more apt description.

His opinion was based upon an examination of the medical records of NDEers. According to his research, many people who had NDEs were not actually close to death.

I disagreed with Dr. Stevenson's findings and said so in a letter that was published in *Lancet*. Stevenson was dealing with a classic problem in near-death studies, namely how does one define "near death"?

As even Zaleski points out, the point of death is hard to define. Death often occurs in tiny pieces without one great dramatic event. And now in modern times, the point of death can no longer be defined because of life support machinery.

As a physician I know firsthand that the moment of death is hard to define. But I look at it in a different way than either Zaleski or Stevenson. If a patient feels that they are near death, and they have a disease or injury from which it is conceivable that they might suffer death, then they should be considered near death. Perhaps in many cases, the patient knows more about how close to death they actually are than theologians and psychiatrists who review their medical records.

The fact that NDEs happen to people who cannot be documented as clinically near death has been known for many years. One of the oldest modern collections of near-death experiences comes from the *Journal of the Swiss Alpine Club* in the late 1800s. Members of the club recorded several dozen experiences of mountain climbers who fell from great heights and yet survived. Just as people whose hearts are restarted, they described stepping out of their physical bodies, floating in peaceful clouds, and having a sense of freedom and peace. Yet these climbers were not physically harmed at all.

Their long falls placed them extremely close to death without causing bodily harm.

There are only two possible explanations for the near-death experience:

- The NDE is a falsification, something that a person unconsciously makes up after being seriously ill. If this is the case, there is no use in beating around the bush in talking about NDEs being a cultural embellishment or a product of religious imagination. If they are made up after the fact, their credibility as real experiences is destroyed. If that is the case, it is a matter for psychologists to explain why people need to invent such tales after the stress of nearly dying.
- Or, NDEs occur to patients at the time that they subjectively say it does, namely at the point of near death or critical illness. I believe that this is the case. I have seen too many people come out of coma or deep unconsciousness talking about traveling up tunnels and seeing bright lights. They never had time to make up a story. And in many cases, they came out of comas, a condition that should "wipe clean the content of man's consciousness," according to textbooks on the subject.

In these cases, the near-death experience at the very least indicates that man has some very exciting and unknown aspects of mental functioning that neuroscience is only beginning to explore.

After listening to hundreds of near-death experiences I will say without hesitation that they are real. They happen to people who do not watch Geraldo, do not read the *National Enquirer*, and who do not have relatives asking them if they saw God when they had their cardiac arrest. In fact, it has only been in the last five years that NDEs have become the focus of mainstream media. How do the skeptics explain the millions of NDEs reported by a wide variety of people before then? These are not secondhand tales passed down through the media. These are firsthand accounts told by people who are puzzled by the experiences they have had.

To tell a patient who has almost died that they did not sit in the lap of Christ even though they vividly described the experience is a form of patient negligence. The medical community sometimes cannot cope with things that have little or no scientific explanation.

The Transformations study has shown that these experiences are so profound that they make real and life-long changes in the people who have them. Even beyond that, the Transformations study has shown that near-death experiences make changes in people who do not even know they have had them.

Our study proved this point by looking at people who were not "culturally biased," which means they did not know they had had a near-death experience until they read *Closer to the Light* or heard me talking about NDEs on radio or television. They knew they had had a brush with death and that "something" had happened, but they had spoken to few people about it and did not have a name for it all of these years.

These were not dreams or tall tales they were telling. These were not reactions to anesthetics or bad dreams resulting from high fever. Their stories were linked to all other near-death experiences by a consistency we call the "core experience." It was amazing to see this consistency of experience in seventy-, eighty-, and even ninety-year-olds who bravely took a step forward for the Transformations study. It is interesting that these adults still remember the pure near-death experience that they had so many years ago and do not further embellish it over the years. If they had their experience as a child, they speak of it in very simple language, almost as though they were children once again. Unlike ordinary memories, NDEs are not embellished over the years.

REAL STORIES

"I began bleeding badly after the birth of my daughter and I was instantly surrounded by medical staff who started working on me. I was in great pain.

"Then suddenly the pain was gone and I was looking down on them working on me. I heard one doctor say he couldn't find a pulse.

"Next I was traveling down a tunnel toward a bright light. But I never reached the end of the tunnel. A gentle voice told me I had to go back. Then I met a dear friend, a neighbor from a town that we had left. He also told me to go back.

"I hit the hospital bed with an electrifying jerk and the pain was back. I was being rushed into an operating theater for surgery to stop the bleeding.

"It was three weeks later that my husband decided I was well enough to be told that my dear friend in that other town had died in an accident on the day my daughter was born."

—A 50-year-old woman

"My wife and I had been told that she couldn't have any more children. But then, in June 1959, I was involved in a serious pit accident at a coal mine. I was taken to the hospital and found to be dead on arrival. But somehow I was revived and remained in a coma for a week.

"While unconscious I had a vision of walking along the sun's rays and seeing a hand with a long white sleeve reaching down. I was almost touching the hand when I felt myself being pulled back, and I heard a voice say: 'Don't worry. You are going to be all right and your son will be all right.'

"A few months later we learned my wife was pregnant and our son was born almost a year to the day after my accident."

—A 66-year-old man

"I was rushed to the hospital as a child, after a bad fall while playing in a derelict building. During the night after I had been unconscious, I felt myself float out of my body and looking down at myself I was convinced I was dead.

"Somebody came toward me and a voice told me it was my father, who had died before I was born. His arms were outstretched and there was a line in front of him. I was sobbing and realized that if I crossed that line there would be no going back. I had the choice and I knew I had nothing to fear, but thinking of my mother and brother, I went back.

"I called for a hospital nurse and told her about it, but she seemed to think it was something to do with the medication."

—A 56-year-old man

"When I was ten years old, I fell off a horse and was knocked out for several hours. The doctor said I might not make it and I saw him say it! It was the oddest thing. I just seemed to pop out of my body! Oh it was just marvelous. I had the greatest fun floating around looking at everybody and myself! Then a lady came who glowed all white. She told me I had to go back home, but that I would come back someday."

—A 90-year-old man

"I didn't really know I had a childhood near-death experience until I heard Dr. Morse speak at a conference. And when he talked about children's NDEs being very simple I thought that probably covered mine.

"I was about eight years old. I had to have some teeth pulled under anesthesia and as I was put to sleep I seemed to be two people. One of me was laying on the operating table and another was rolled up into a ball being hurled very fast through a long, dark tunnel. The doctor said later that he had given me too much ether and my heart had stopped. I guess that's when I split in two. It all seemed very simple."

—A 56-year-old woman

"My NDE happened in 1960. I had just had a baby and I felt sick. The doctor said I was just having the 'baby blues' but I just didn't buy it. I told them I felt funny and wanted to stay in the hospital for a few days longer and they said okay. They thought it was nothing, but I knew something was going to happen.

"It finally did happen about five one morning. I had a blood clot in my legs that moved into one of my lungs and stopped my heart. That happened when a nurse came by with my baby. I sat up in bed and swung my legs out when I just passed out. I slid to the floor and then I was enveloped in total blackness.

"I saw myself on the floor by the bed. I could see a lot of details. For example, my gown had slid up around my waist and one of the nurses was trying to pull it down to cover me. There was no piped-in oxygen and I saw an orderly drag a tank of the stuff into the room. I heard the nurse screaming, 'Call the doctor, call her husband, call a priest,' stuff like that. And then I saw somebody lift my body and put it on the bed. That was when I realized that I was out of my body.

"I floated close and looked down. I knew I wasn't on that pillow. I could see a body there and its hair was wet and strung out on the pillow, its eyes were closed and the lips were blue.

"But I wasn't there. I was floating up near the ceiling.

"My hearing became extremely acute. I heard and saw other patients on the floor. One was across the hall. She was talking to a nurse and complaining of the noise that was coming from my room. I saw another doctor that I had known since childhood come to the nursing desk that was way down the hall. She told him what was happening and he said, "I better call her mother," which I later found out he did.

"In the meantime, I felt just wonderful. I felt no pain. I felt like an observer, floating there between two worlds, one that I knew well and one that I didn't know existed.

"In time it seemed as though the ceiling was paved with blue/white clouds, and the air seemed sprinkled with gold dust.

"It became very bright and I found myself standing at the entrance to—not a tunnel—but a sort of very long canopy like you might see going into a nightclub. It was as though it were made of blue and silver rays and the canopy arched and reached down to the cloud path on either side. The powerful light was on the other end of the canopy.

"Now I didn't see anyone there or talk to anyone, but I felt that there were other presences. And I felt that they were real happy and joyous with the anticipation of my coming.

"I looked down to the room again and saw the doctors and nurses working on the patient, who was me. I saw that the patient didn't struggle to breathe and really didn't seem to move at all.

"A priest came in and he said, 'I'll pray for her soul.' A nurse came in from another floor and stood at the foot of my bed. She said: 'I don't think she's going to make it. It's too bad. She is only twenty-five.'

"I became aware of a soft crying in the hall. I recognized my husband who was talking to his aunt and saying, 'What can I tell the children?' His aunt, who is a nurse, was sitting stooped over with her back against the wall, saying, 'She was such a good little mother.'

"That I could see all of this proved I was out of my body. These people were all outside the room and down the hall so I couldn't have seen it from the bed.

"I knew that body was mine and all I felt for it was sympathy. I tried to tell people in the room that I wasn't in pain and I wished that they could be up there with me. Then I just sort of relaxed. I felt privileged to see something that they weren't able to understand or see.

"Then one of them started banging on my chest with all of his might and I opened my eyes.

"For several days after that I just stared at the ceiling. They say I did that for about three days. I think I was waiting to see those stars or for that other world to open up again.

"I have thought about this experience a lot, but didn't know that it has happened to anyone else until I heard about it on the radio. I was glad to hear that there are other people just like me."

—A 57-year-old woman

All these experiences took place long before discussion of near-death experiences became mainstream. All were laden with core experiences. And best of all, none of these people even knew NDEs existed until recently.

Should these people be told that their near-death experiences are not real? Not to my way of thinking.

THE CORE EXPERIENCE

But we shouldn't forget about the woman who saw Elvis in the light, should we? As one skeptic pointed out, "If these experiences are real and not just dreams, how can you explain Elvis?" Or Buddha? How can NDEs of children be explained where they see pet dogs, or elementary school teachers who are still alive? They show up in some NDEs too. How can they be explained?

By studying the experiences of children I learned the answer to this puzzle. Simply stated it is this: There is a core near-death experience (a sense of leaving one's body, traveling up a tunnel, seeing people of light, etc.) which is shared by all ages and cultures. Along with those core experiences come secondary embellishments, descriptions of various details and figures that come from a person's personal and cultural background. These are emotional archetypes incorporated into the experience by the beholder to help make sense of it.

So when the woman in the Midwest saw Elvis, she was probably projecting him onto the bright light that others have described as God or Buddha or have been unable to describe at all. Meeting Elvis as a child may have inspired the same awe and respect she felt when she met the light as an adult. Yet the persistence of the core experience demonstrates that the entire experience is not embellished.

Let me give you some other examples of cultural embellishment, first in other cultures and then in my own study.

FROM DEEPEST AFRICA

Dr. Nsama Mumbwe of the University of Zambia in Africa became fascinated by near-death experiences as a result of reading *Closer to the Light*. Wondering if NDEs are just an American phenomenon born of media coverage, she decided to search for people in her own culture who had had this experience themselves. She found fifteen near-death experiencers through patient records and physician referrals. Among them was a dentist, a truck driver, a charcoal burner, housewives, a grandmother, and a miner. In short, she had a good cross section of this society.

All of them had had near-fatal illnesses or accidents. All of them were asked standard personal questions and then were asked to describe the experience itself. After that they were asked questions about their belief, what the experience meant to them.

These are people who, in most cases, do not have

television, radio, or newspapers. They are simple people who had never heard of a near-death experience so certainly couldn't make one up. Yet every one of the fifteen subjects found by Dr. Mumbwe in Lusaka, Zambia, had the same core experiences as NDEers in other parts of the world. These people in this remote Third World country have the same near-death experiences as people who were in my study. To me these case studies once again prove the validity of the NDE as an actual experience described as it happened and not made up later. That is not to say there are not cultural differences. In the case studies you are about to read, note that some of the people think that they were being bewitched during the experience. Even though the experience was the same as we have recorded in the United States, many of these African people interpreted the event as somewhat evil. Half of the participants in this simple study thought the NDE signified that they were "bewitched" or about to be. Another called it a "bad omen."

Here are some of Dr. Mumbwe's fascinating case studies:

"I had sustained a fractured femur and a head injury after an accident. I was unconscious for a day. I believed that I had died. I went to a place where I found a lot of people dressed in white robes—children and adults. I couldn't make out their races. These people seemed to be very happy. But then when I appeared they stopped singing and someone said, 'We were not expecting you. Sorry!'

"I hurried 'round and left. I could hear them start their singing after I had walked a good distance from them.

"[My belief is that] someone must have been trying to bewitch me but found me innocent."

—A 35-year-old clerk

"I was attacked by a lioness in the bush. I had seen beautiful cubs behind a shrub and without much thinking I tried to catch one of the cubs.

"Suddenly from behind me came the lioness leaping in the midair. Before I realized what was happening, the lioness had dug its claws into the right side of my chest and was beginning to tear me apart.

"Fortunately my elder brother who was with me threw a spear coated with some poison at the lioness. It struck the lioness right in the throat. The lioness suddenly became limp and fell to the ground.

"My brother came to my side and tied the wound up with his shirt to arrest bleeding. He asked me if I was all right. As I was trying to say, 'yes,' I could see myself going into some kind of a trance. A highway suddenly opened up before me. It seemed to be going endlessly into the sky. Along it were a lot of stars, also spreading up to the sky.

"Each time I tried to get on the highway the stars would block my way. I just stood there not knowing what to do. After a while the highway and stars disappeared. I woke up and found myself in a hospital bed.

"[I believe] it was a bad omen, because when my brother got home he found my mother very ill and she died the next day."

—A 60-year-old truck driver

"I was suffering from a stroke. During this time I felt I was put into a big calabash [the hollow shell of a gourd] with a big opening. But somehow I couldn't get out of it. Then a voice from somewhere said to me, 'Be brave. Take my hand and come out. It is not yet your time to go.'

"After some time of being in the calabash I managed to get out on my own.

"I believe someone was trying to bewitch me, but found that I was an innocent soul."

—An 85-year-old grandmother of six

"I was unconscious for three days when I was being treated for malaria. My experience during this time was that I saw two people, a man and a woman. They said it was not time for me to die and that I should go back home to my people and that they would come again to take me.

"I believe it was not my time to die and that someone had tried to bewitch me into death but these two people stopped it."

—A 50-year-old widow with three children

NOTE: Patient died early January 1990. According to the sister who was there at the time of her death, she said the patient was talking about two people who had come to take her.

"I had collapsed in my village house and was assumed dead for three days. I was lucky not to have been buried because they were waiting for my son to arrive.

"During this time of collapse, I had gone on a long journey. I heard people talking in different languages. I couldn't however make out what they were saying.

"Then someone spoke to me in my language—Bemba. He

said, 'You have come a day earlier than we expected you. Please go back.' Later I recovered from my unconsciousness.

"I think it wasn't my time to die."

—A 60-year-old charcoal burner

These cases from Dr. Mumbwe carry with them certain cultural beliefs. Some of these people speak of going to witch doctors to get rid of the curse. Others don't think they were bewitched, but their families do. Some put no spiritual belief on what happened. Instead they treat the experience as though they walked into the wrong house and were simply asked to leave.

Yet, although they are on the other side of the world, their NDEs are essentially the same, exhibiting the same core elements of going up tunnels, seeing people dressed in white, and so forth. They interpret them differently, because of their culture.

BEWITCHED AND BEWILDERING

Sometimes the experience is bewitching to people here, too. Perhaps "bewildering" is a better word. This is especially true when the near-death experience goes against the person's belief system.

Take Jamie, for instance. She was very disturbed by her experience. Her moment of near death came as a result of bacterial meningitis. Her fever soared and her vital signs plummeted. At one point she was resuscitated by a physician who gave her only a 10-percent chance of living.

During resuscitation she left her body and watched

the doctors and nurses "doing a lot of stuff to me," which I assume meant lifesaving procedures. Then, as Jamie describes it:

"Suddenly, everything went all dark and I was scared. I floated up and I was in heaven. There was a huge rainbow and there were dead people. You know, people waiting to be born. And I talked to Jesus."

I was curious. "What was Jesus like?" I asked.

"Oh he was nice," she said. Then she clammed up and didn't say another word. I could see that she was disturbed.

"Can you describe more of Jesus?" I asked.

She seemed uncomfortable at the request. He was in a very bright light that she could not describe other than by saying that it made her feel good. He was sitting there with a round belly and a red hat, looking like Santa Claus. She saw him, she said, and even spoke to him just as she was speaking to me. He told her that everything would be okay and that she would have to go back to her body and grow up. After he said that, she found herself back in the hospital.

Her experience seemed pleasant enough to me. After telling a story like this, children are usually relaxed, but the experience had obviously frightened Jamie. In fact, her mother had brought her to me because Jamie had been moody and uncommunicative since the NDE. Right now she seemed downright frightened.

I pried harder. "Why are you so scared?" I asked.

"Because I went to heaven and saw Jesus," she blurted out. "I didn't think you were supposed to be able to talk to Jesus. And if I was really in heaven, why did I come back? I didn't think we are supposed to see heaven and still be alive."

She sat there a few seconds and then cut right to the most crucial question of all. "Was it real?" she asked. "Did it really happen to me? It didn't seem like a dream. It seemed realer than real. I really went to heaven and talked to Jesus—didn't I?"

I told her that it was not a dream and assured her that she was sane. She would have to decide exactly what the experience meant to her.

She seemed to relax. She was very aware that many elements of her near-death experience did not match with things she had been taught in Sunday school. For one, the pictures of Jesus she saw hanging on the church walls did not show him wearing a red hat and having a round belly like Santa. For another, she was taught that heaven was where people go when they die. So why had she seen people about to be born? Although she was only seven, she understood that people who claim to talk to God are considered crazy in our society. In fact, it was precisely because her near-death experience did not fit her religious and cultural perceptions that it was so disturbing!

Jamie's experience carried with it certain cultural embellishments. Perhaps she felt the same nervousness and comfort with the light that she did when looking at pictures of Christ in books or when she sat on Santa's lap in a department store. Perhaps the comfort she felt was somehow visually projected upon the mystical light that engulfed her. Perhaps what she saw was part of a past life review that represented snippets of her life that she didn't fully recognize. Perhaps she was having a past life review and wasn't able to identify it because she didn't know enough about near-death experiences.

A UNIQUE FINGERPRINT

The doubt, the questions, the argument will go on forever with some people. I am convinced that NDEs are real. I can also say that the NDE leaves a unique fingerprint on a person that cannot be duplicated by any other experience, especially dreams and hallucinations. The NDE, especially the experience of seeing the mystical light, changes lives forever.

People can't make up changes like that.

Still, beyond the core experience there is some cultural diversity in near-death experiences. Beyond the common elements like leaving the body, seeing angelic people or dead relatives, having a life review, and experiencing a warm and loving light, there is often some element of the person's culture that shows up.

In Japan, a study of four hundred near-death experiencers reveals that many of them see long dark rivers and beautiful flowers. Indians sometimes see heaven as a giant bureaucracy and are frequently sent back because of clerical errors. Americans and the English are usually sent back for love or to do a job while the natives of Micronesia say that the heaven they see is similar to a large, brightly lit American city with loud noisy cars and tall buildings.

Are all of these experiences different? On the whole I say no. The reason for this diverse interpretation is that the near-death experience is ultimately a mystical experience that cannot be described. This bright light that comes to us at the point of death and the events leading up to it are unlike anything we have previously experienced. What NDEers have seen is not abstract imagery. It is very clearly tunnels and people of light. But it is also a different reality. And because of that, as humans we struggle to explain what has happened and in doing so draw on our only resources: words and the world as we know it. Sometimes we cannot even do that.

This is best demonstrated by a six-year-old girl who could not talk, yet related her near-death experience to her parents.

She was in a car accident in which she received severe head injuries. The damage to her brain affected her ability to control her tongue and to swallow. These problems, coupled with a tracheotomy hole in her neck to help with her breathing, prevented her from talking. Yet despite those problems, she could understand everything that was said to her.

Soon after the accident, she insisted on bringing her parents into the hospital chapel. There she pointed to a picture of Jesus that was framed on the wall. Then she pointed to a ray of light streaming in from a partially closed window. She clapped and smiled and pointed to the ray of light and Jesus. She pantomimed traveling down a long tunnel for her parents.

This child clearly had a near-death experience and showed it to her parents in a vivid and unmistakable fashion. Yet since she could not speak, she had to use the world around her to describe what she saw. Although some might consider her description to be full of secondary embellishments, the little girl certainly got her point across.

6

The Circuit Boards of Mysticism

"Mystical consciousness is a state of insight into the depths of truth unplumbed by the discussive intellect."
—*William James*

I met a man who was deeply disturbed by an experience he had as a combat soldier in Vietnam. I was able to comfort him simply by noticing that he did not wear a wristwatch. Here is his experience:

"I was wounded by shrapnel and fell unconscious in the mud. My face was flat down and I began to suffocate. I knew what was happening. I was bleeding and dazed (probably in shock) but instead of it being agonizing, it actually felt very peaceful. I felt a great calm that, given the fighting that went on just moments before, is amazing.

"I felt very much at peace there in the mud. Then suddenly, I was floating out of my body and looking at myself. I could see my stomach wounds, the blood, my messed up hair, but I had no concern for myself. I was worried about my family. I didn't want them to see me like this, all bloody and messy.

139

I felt sad that my mother might see me but other than that I wasn't overly concerned, given the situation

"Out of the corner of my eye I saw two figures. They were guys I knew. They had also died but they were out of their bodies like I was. They started to walk away.

"They motioned for me to come with them but I felt sad for my mother and felt that I couldn't leave my body. They nodded to me. They seemed to know how I felt and they simply waved good-bye. I then saw a medic turn my head so my face was uncovered. Suddenly I was in my body and breathing again."

Although the experience had affected him profoundly throughout the years, many people tried to convince him that it wasn't real. His brother said it was a bad dream, even though he had never described it in "bad" terms. Some friends acted as though he had made the incident up. His wife at one time even threatened to leave him if he continued to talk about what had happened. She said he was like a different person, one who seemed to be on a spiritual quest to understand his experience.

He went to a doctor who examined his wounds and insisted that they had not been serious enough to put him near death. To me this sort of argument is senseless. All physicians who work in critical-care medicine can tell you that it is extremely difficult to predict who is going to live or die based upon their clinical course. Some patients seem certain to die, and instead make a full recovery against all odds. Others seem to be recovering and take a sudden turn and die. One of the strange realities of the intensive-care unit is that the patient least discussed during morning rounds is the one most likely to "crash" that night. It is hard to figure out who is going to live or die when we physicians are at the bedside. I feel I can categorically state that no one can review medical records at a later date and say who was close to death and who was not. This man was wounded, dazed, and drowning in mud, a combination of factors that sound like near-death to me. Now his life was upside down. He was already plagued with guilt about living while his buddies had died around him. He was already wondering, as so many people do, if his experience was real. Why torture him further by looking at his wounds and declaring that he was never near death? What happened to him conflicted so much with the beliefs of those around him that he was being forced to devalue his own vivid and real experience, one that was a mix of horror, grief, guilt, and wondrous spirituality. In short, he was in a state of spiritual emergency.

This man came to me out of need. My advice was simple. Do not denigrate the experience or let anyone else do so. I told him about a parent who, upon listening to their child tell of his near-death experience, said: "Don't listen to him. He has always had a great imagination."

This kind of response is degrading and cruel. All mystical experiences conflict with the "real world." That is their very nature. To devalue them is cynical and even ignorant.

"You certainly aren't crazy and the experience certainly did happen," I told the man. "Learn from it, don't *lean* from it."

I was slipping into my best rhetoric when I noticed

something. *This man wasn't wearing a watch!* My train of thought changed abruptly.

"Why don't you wear a watch?" I asked him.

"I don't know," he said. "To tell you the truth, they never work right for me. They always just quit running."

WATCH-STOPPING EXPERIENCE

That was all I needed to hear to assure him that his experience was definitely real. Although I do not know there is life after death and I don't know where his buddies were going when they waved good-bye, I do know that more than one-fourth of all adults who survived near-death experiences as children said that they could not wear watches. The reason? They simply stopped running.

One-fourth of a study population that mysteriously stops watches is astonishing, especially when compared to the other groups we studied. Only 4 percent of normal adults, those who had never had an NDE or a paranormal experience, found that they could not wear watches without having them stop running. Four percent of those who survived childhood illnesses could not wear watches without breaking them, while 2 percent of the people who had had spontaneous out-of-body experiences found themselves unable to wear timepieces.

We discovered this remarkable correlation by asking a simple question: *Do you have difficulties wearing watches or problems with lights or electrical appliances?*

The people who answered yes were interviewed

about the type of problems they have. One man had purchased three watches during the past five years only to have each of them fail in succession. The remarkable thing, he said, was that they ran again without having to be repaired when he gave them to his sons. Another man keeps his two-hundred-dollar watch tucked into a corner of his dresser drawer. He finds it peculiar that the watch stops when he puts it on his wrist, but runs fine when it's in the drawer. "I guess the batteries are messed up," he says.

Actually I do not think it is the watch batteries that are messed up. After scientifically studying hundreds of these experiences I am convinced that the NDE itself subtly changes the electromagnetic forces that surround our bodies and each and every cell in it. This change is so profound that it affects such things as personality, anxiety response, ability to have psychic experiences, and even the ability in some to wear a watch.

POWERFUL INTERNAL FORCE

This electromagnetic force field is not science fiction. It has been used to heal broken bones and even regenerate limbs on some animals. Changes in these electromagnetic fields have been associated with tumor growth and regression. This force is considered by many experts to represent a promising avenue of cancer treatment. Medical science has seen it with the help of sensitive machines. In fact we even use it with a whole new generation of "imaging" devices that allow us to look at the heart and other organs without using the radiation of X rays or cutting people open. These devices work by detecting the slightest changes in this force field, and translating those changes into pictures with photographic clarity.

This subtle force field can even be seen by some who report seeing auras or halos around people. It can certainly be "seen" with X-ray machines, and has been captured on film by a number of radiologists. A few researchers are now experimenting with the effect that this force field has on personality, thoughts, and emotions. Some researchers even claim that by altering this force field they can cure addictions and phobias. A few psychologists have even built successful practices doing just that.

I believe this subtle and powerful electromagnetic field is permanently altered by the near-death experience. This field interacts with the body and functions as a second nervous system. After considerable research, which I will share with you, I feel it is safe to say that electrical changes are responsible for the transformations we see in near-death experiencers. In short, people who have near-death experiences are "rewired."

The NDE changes our "I am," the inner sense of consciousness, that aspect of ourselves we consider to be unique. It shows itself in many ways: decreased death anxiety, less desire for material goods, greater spiritualism, an occasional ability to heal, and many more paranormal experiences. In a large number of people there is such a profound change that their electromagnetic signature can actually stop a watch.

How is it possible that an experience of light at the point of death can result in something so bizarre as not being able to wear a watch? And why does this happen only to those who nearly die? In order to understand this, we must first review the startling research in both physics and medicine that explains the role of electromagnetism in our lives. Most of this research has been conducted in just the last twenty years and helps explain many of the mysteries of the world.

For more than two hundred years now, we have viewed the universe as mechanical. Sir Isaac Newton likened the planets to billiard balls that move around each other with precision and predictability.

Likewise, modern medicine was founded on understandings of chemical and molecular actions that occur within the body. As with the universe, atoms and molecules are seen essentially as billiard balls too, their interactions determining the biological processes of life.

This marvelous view has made it possible to understand the workings of the human body. Medicines are composed of molecules that interact in predictable ways to kill germs and viruses. Now we can even alter genes to cure birth defects that are part of our genetic makeup.

Molecules that make up our body, like Newton's universe, are made of atoms circling atoms in a predictable fashion. Each molecule is a universe unto itself. These molecules communicate with each other and grow together into specialized parts to make human beings and everything around us. For instance, the paper on this page is as solid as it looks, but it is composed of billions of tiny molecules that in turn are composed of countless atoms. And *those* are composed of electrons, neutrons, and protons.

That has been the accepted view of matter—until

about fifty years ago. Then science discovered an even smaller world than the electron. They call this tiny world wave/particle duality. According to astrophysicist Stephen Hawking, it works like this: As physicists have split the atom into smaller and smaller particles, they have discovered to their surprise that there is no final "tiniest part" of nature. Rather, there are forces best described as wavelengths of electromagnetism, or light. These pieces of light serve as the fundamental building blocks for everything. What this theory tells us is that everything we consider to be real actually breaks down into simple light, in all of its various wavelengths. This is the same message that came from many NDEers in the study. As one patient said: "I could see the light in all my own cells and in the universe. I could see that light was God."

Although this theory may sound like a bunch of scientific doublespeak, especially to anyone who has stubbed their toe on a solid object, it has led to many of the scientific advances of the computer age.

For instance the imaging machines that I mentioned earlier provide pictures of body parts by "seeing" their unique electromagnetic signatures. These instruments once required radioactivity to see inside us. Now many of them are so sensitive that they can just use the naturally occurring electromagnetism.

If someone had predicted twenty years ago that the X ray would eventually be replaced by instruments that would detect the natural magnetic resonance of living cells, they would have been ridiculed. Yet now no one blinks an eye when such things are mentioned. As Stephen Hawking says: "We have come to recognize that events cannot be predicted with complete accuracy but that there is always a degree of uncertainty. If one likes, one can ascribe this uncertainty to the intervention of God."

DUAL NERVOUS SYSTEM

Human beings have a dual nervous system, one composed of nerve impulses and the other of electric currents. The ways in which these electromagnetic forces interact with the world are well documented. Birds, for example, have sensitive magnets within their brains that sense the earth's electromagnetic fields and use that information like a compass to tell direction. Some fish have electromagnetic sensors that orient them to the bottom of the ocean, helping them to know which end is up. Many fish have electromagnetic sensors which locate other fish. Electric eels go a step further. Not only can they sense the electromagnetic fields of other fish, they can harness their own electromagnetic energy to shock and stun these fish. Most animals have an area in the brain which can sense electromagnetic forces. The salamander has two such organs which it uses for navigation. And humans have one, an area behind the ethmoid sinuses that was discovered by Dr. Robin Baker of the University of Manchester in England.

This ability to sense electromagnetic fields has important clinical implications. Solar storms, which generate bursts of electromagnetic radiation, have been shown to affect human behavior to such an extent that they increase admissions to psychiatric hospitals. Researcher Frank Brown of Woods Hole Marine Biological Laboratory has shown that natural biorhythms, sleep cycles, and patterns of behavior are all influenced by the earth's magnetic fields.

Even cancer has sometimes been shown to be caused—and healed—by electromagnetism from outside the body. In a sobering study, Dr. Nancy Westheimer of the University of Colorado showed that 20 percent of childhood cancers are caused by force fields radiated from overhead power lines. The New York State Department of Health conducted its own power-line study and reached the same conclusion. Dr. Wendell Winters of the University of Texas has shown that electromagnetism from power lines depresses the human immune system and stimulates the growth of some cancers. And Dr. Marjorie Speers, also of the University of Texas, documented that utility workers and linemen exposed to power-line magnetic fields have a thirteenfold increase in brain tumors.

Power-line electromagnetism has been linked to an increase in suicides and a decrease in neurochemicals serotonin and dopamine which control such things as sleep and mood. Dr. Jose Delgado has dramatically demonstrated the role that electromagnetism can play in mood by planting an electrode in a bull's brain. On national television, he stopped the bull dead in its tracks by signaling the electrode with a hand-held transmitter. The resulting change in the brain chemistry turned the rampaging bull into a gentle pussycat. He was also able to induce rage or sleep in monkeys through similar electromagnetic stimulation.

CURED BY THE LIGHT

One such case to illustrate the healing potential of the light comes from a thirty-nine-year-old woman in the study whom I will call Janet. She was not among those in the study group who had had a near-death experience. Rather, she was in the group of people who had been under severe stress and had had a mystical experience of light.

She had been diagnosed with basal cell carcinoma, a form of skin cancer. The cancerous lesion was on her nose and her doctors insisted that she have it removed immediately. As she tells it:

"I was in the deepest state of depression and despair that I have ever known.

"Two nights before surgery I was sleeping when I was awakened by a bright light shining in my eyes. I opened my eyes to see a large sphere of light floating about five feet in front of me. There was a light within it that was rotating slowly from left to right. This sphere spoke to me: 'You aren't afraid, are you?'

"Seeing this light made me fearless. In fact I was filled with the most incredible peace I have ever known. Whoever was speaking to me knew what all my problems and fears were. All of my burdens slipped away.

"Suddenly the light went through me. It didn't reflect off of me or anything like that. It went straight through me. As it did, I was filled with unconditional love which was so complete and powerful that I would need to invent new words to describe it.

"I asked that my cancer would be removed. I prayed actually. And the light said that what we think of as prayer is more like complaining and we are frequently begging to be punished for something that we are simply going to do again in the future.

"He asked me to think of my own worst enemy and I did. Then he said to send all of my light to my worst enemy. I did and a sudden burst of light went out of me and returned as if it had been reflected back from a mirror. I became aware of every cell in my body. I could see every cell in my body. It was the sound and sight of light coming from my being. I was crying, laughing, shaking, trying to hold still and trying to catch my breath. When I finally recovered, the being of light said, 'now you have prayed for the first time in your life.' "

I am intrigued by this experience of light for a number of reasons. First and foremost, Janet's cancer disappeared. It is extremely rare for a basal cell carcinoma simply to disappear.

Although no one has documented that the use of magnetic fields can cure cancer, it is certainly scientifically respectable to state that changes in the body's electromagnetic field are linked to tumor growth and regression.

Just as important in its own way, this experience is proof of the realness of the mystical experience. Through the stress and fear of her life-threatening condition she tapped into the circuit boards of mysticism that reside in the right temporal lobe. This is the area that is activated by the near-death experience as well as other mystical experiences like the one that Janet had.

I do believe that this woman, through fear and stress similar to that experienced by people on the brink of death, altered her own electromagnetic forces and was able spontaneously to regress this cancerous lesion.

Electromagnetism from outside our bodies can be used to heal broken bones. Dr. Robert Becker, an orthopedic surgeon and professor of medicine at Syracuse University in New York, has pioneered the use of electromagnetic forces to help heal fractures that cannot be healed in any other way. His work has led to the healing of breaks in thousands of patients who otherwise would have been permanently crippled. Interestingly enough, electricity was first used in the early 1800s to heal broken bones. Since it conflicted with traditional views of medicine, no one really worked with the healing properties of electricity until Becker revived interest in the last two decades.

Becker and others have been able to use electric currents to quickly induce the regeneration of entire limbs in mice and salamanders in a laboratory setting using carefully controlled amounts of electricity. There are also some cases in the medical literature of spontaneous regeneration, body parts that grow back on their own, without outside stimulation.

One such example comes from Australia, where doctors in the Flying Doctor service report that they have seen children grow fingers back that were severed in an accident. They found that if they cleaned the stump of a severed finger and left it open, it would sometimes regrow in a matter of weeks, complete with new bone and fingernail. But if they sewed up the wound, the appendage would never grow back.

Becker and others credit this regeneration to the

body's own electromagnetic forces, which they consider a sort of master control.

GROWING NEW LIMBS

Dr. Becker has brilliantly demonstrated that regeneration is controlled by electromagnetic forces in his work on salamanders. As mentioned, he has been able to use electric currents to induce the regeneration of the entire limbs of salamanders. To test this master control theory he transplanted some of these regenerated limbs from the front of the salamanders to the back. If regeneration was simply a mechanical process, he reasoned, then the transplanted forelimb should continue to *look* like a forelimb. It would be similar to a human's arm being switched with their leg.

What happened was remarkable. The transplanted forelimb turned into a hind limb. If the salamander's genes alone were responsible for growth, then the transplanted limb should have continued to look like a hand. This was obviously not just a mechanical process. A new hind limb was needed and the change was made. Was this determining force electromagnetic?

Becker went a step further to find out. He interfered with the electromagnetic force field in the brains of the salamanders. All forms of regeneration stopped.

I mention these studies to demonstrate that this "unseen power" has in fact been well researched. As a result of the Transformations study, I too consider these electromagnetic forces a sort of master control that contributes to such things as mood, attitude, anxiety, and even paranormal events like healings, telepathy, precognition, and seeing ghosts. In fact paranormal may be considered quite normal as future studies unveil more information about this incredible unseen nervous system.

Let me give an example of a spontaneous healing of cancer, and how a near-death experience may have led to it.

CURED OF CANCER

A woman I shall call Kathy certainly thinks it did. She is a reserved forty-five-year-old mother of three who runs her own business. More than ten years ago she was diagnosed as having cancer of the thyroid gland. After radiation and chemotherapy treatments, her doctor told her that the cancer had spread to other parts of her body and she probably had only six months to live.

She left her business in the hands of others, went home with her family, wrote out her will, settled her affairs, and waited to die.

Her weakened immune system left her vulnerable to infection. Within a few weeks she developed viral pneumonia and was readmitted to the hospital. Despite best efforts, Kathy's illness became worse and worse. One night her breathing and heart stopped. Doctors rushed into her room to start life-saving procedures.

Here's the story as Kathy tells it:

"Everything went very dark for a few seconds. Then suddenly I was way high on top of a ridge, overlooking a beautiful valley. The colors were extremely vivid, far more vivid than those I have previously experienced. It was marvelous. I was filled with a thrilling sense of joy.

"A being was at my side, a being of light. Yet it wasn't like a light that you see, but rather felt and understood. It touched me, and my whole body was filled with its light. It was bursting out of me. I sensed a voice telling me that I could not enter this wonderful valley, that my children still needed me."

Almost miraculously, Kathy recovered from the pneumonia and her cardiac arrest to experience another miracle a few weeks later. Her cancer disappeared.

She immediately thought the healing was caused by the powerful experience of light she had had during her near-death experience. Her doctor doubted the connection. He said it was probably caused by a jolt to her immune system caused by the severity of her illness.

When Kathy came into the study she told me her story and then asked what I thought: "Did the near-death experience cure my cancer or was it done by my immune system?"

Looking at all the data compiled on the subject, including the proximity of the near-death experience to the healing, I find it hard to believe that the NDE did not have a direct influence on the cancer.

Numerous scientific studies have documented that the growth and regression of cancerous cells can be accomplished by electromagnetic force fields of different intensities. These force fields have also been shown to affect the performance of the pineal gland, a tiny nodule deep in the brain which secretes hormones that influence the working of the immune system. This tiny gland is the remnant third eye in many primitive animals. It doesn't function as a seeing eye in the eels and fish that have it, but one that registers the color of the surroundings so an animal can change its protective coloration.

In the human, the pineal gland is being shown to be responsible for other types of protection. Although it is sunken from the surface and deep into the brain, some cancer researchers feel that it responds to electromagnetic stimulation to boost the immune system.

My feeling is that the brilliant light, the one she described as "bursting" out of her, affected her body's electromagnetism which in turn boosted her immune system. So my answer to her was yes on both counts. The NDE improved her immune system which in turn healed her cancer.

"LIGHT SHOUT" OF CHANGE

Am I basing my opinion just on the results of the Transformations study? Not at all. Although this is a conclusive study with many subjects, a theory like this should not be based on a single study alone. Has anyone else shown that a near-death experience has an effect on a person's electromagnetic fingerprint? Has anyone else shown these experiences of light are more than just visual hallucinations? And is there more research that shows the positive effects of changes in this subtle force field?

The answer to all of this is yes.

First, let us examine the change in the electromagnetic signature. We know that dying organisms emit intense amounts of electromagnetic energy, or light. I was amazed to find just how much light they give off. Physicist Janusz Slawinki, writing in the *Journal of Near-Death Studies*, found that dying organisms emit a "light shout" more than a thousand times greater than their usual resting state. As cells die and genetic material begins to unfold as it does at death, a powerful charge of electromagnetic energy is given off. This light is something NDEers actually see, not a hallucination. On rare occasions *other* people have reported seeing this light radiating from a dying person. This phenomenon has been reported by people who are not emotionally attached to the dying person or who did not even know they were dying.

Such a charge would have a great effect upon the entire body, including the right temporal lobe of the brain, the area directly over your right ear. This is the area I call "the seat of the soul." In previous research we have found that this part of the brain is genetically encoded for the near-death experience. Other researchers have found that it is the area where mystical experiences occur. This may explain how, when the rest of the brain is dying, this area has the energy to function at a higher level than ever before.

The right temporal lobe is the circuit board of mysticism. This area, along with a complex brain organ called the hippocampus, makes us unique from previous species of mankind. In fact, says Nobel Laureate Sir John Eccles, it is not the *size* of our brains that makes us unique as humans, but the presence of the temporal lobes. This is the area responsible for complex language, self-consciousness, long-term planning, daydreams, and soulful thought. It is also our link to consciousness, our link to the divine. It has been called "the man inside the man," by famed neurosurgeon Wilder Penfield, who seemed to be working hard in some of his writings to avoid the word *soul*. One thing is certain though, people who lose this area to surgery or brain damage becomes soulless automatons who act like zombies.

The near-death experience affects this portion of the brain. I feel I can safely say this based upon the large number of provable changes seen in near-death experiencers. Remember, the subjects in the Transformations study had changes in anxiety levels, health status, attitude, and the number of paranormal experiences. Many people reported that it made them more sensitive, or have less fear of death. Many felt it had made them less uptight than their fellow man.

I have plenty of evidence to show changes in the minds of NDEers. After all, any change in personality must involve biochemical changes in the brain. But rather than rely only upon my own study and experience to illustrate this change, I'll show how other researchers have "rewired" this area of the brain and the results they have documented.

ALTERED CURRENTS

One such brain electrician is Dr. Margaret Patterson, a well-known British surgeon who treats alcohol and drug abuse by applying electric currents to the brains of substance abusers. For fifteen years she has done this, applying a weak electrical current adjacent to the temporal lobe.

Dr. Patterson has an extremely high cure rate. The

reason for the cure, she says, is that the technique changes the electrical current of the brain. This is the same area of the brain in which the near-death experience occurs and the results are largely the same: the person is transformed. In fact, one of the reasons she is such a popular doctor is that the cure transforms her patients into nonaddictive personalities, meaning they do not simply replace one addiction with another.

Other researchers who have electrically stimulated the temporal lobes to change behavior have met with much the same levels of success. Many psychotics, for instance, are reportedly transformed for the better by passing electrical current through the temporal lobe. This is not the same as electroshock therapy, which is a powerful jolt of electricity administered to the frontal lobe. Rather, the temporal lobe stimulation is a much smaller dose of electricity that is administered while the patient is conscious.

Perhaps the most interesting theory about this transformation comes from Dr. James Kubie, who links *neurotic* behavior with abnormal currents of electricity in the temporal lobes. He says this behavior is caused by repressed memory that has become closed circuits of neurons. These closed circuits cause nervous energy that leads to neurosis. I suspect that the electromagnetic energy of the near-death experience erases these closed circuits. Based upon the tests in the Transformations study, it is clear that neurotic elements are no longer present.

Some psychologists have reportedly cured addictions and phobias by simply "realigning" the body's electromagnetic force field. Most notable among these innovative psychologists is Dr. Roger Callahan of Palm Springs, California. Callahan believes that all addictions and phobias are caused by a misalignment of the body's electrical system. This misalignment causes a rise in anxiety which a person tries to quell by eating, drinking, or drugging. As a result, they become addicted.

Using a series of techniques that resemble acupressure, Callahan has been able to cure more than 90 percent of the phobics he has treated and over 80 percent of patients with food addictions. His revolutionary work is being researched in a number of university hospitals and is being hailed as a major contribution to addiction research. All of these innovative and useful treatments use the body's own electromagnetic forces to make dramatic changes in behavior. The near-death experience works in much the same way.

A tremendous amount of energy is released during the near-death experience. This energy is generated internally and probably reaches its peak when the person is bathed in the light. Most NDEers are unable to describe this light, but what they are surely seeing is a blast of the energy that powers their life. As one child told me: "I know that other people saw God. But I only saw a light, a light that has everything in it."

This energy is funneled through the right temporal lobe which is altered by the experience. The temporal lobe, in turn, has a profound effect upon the various structures of the brain and the electromagnetic field that surrounds the body.

The person who has a near-death experience may look the same, but their electrochemical makeup is very different from what they used to be.

STILL MYSTERIOUS

On the surface, these concepts seem to devalue the mystical aspects of the near-death experience, but think about it more deeply. Look at it through the eyes of these patients and ask yourself: Is the mystery of the experience diminished or just beginning? Is it time for philosophers and religious thinkers to develop new philosophies that will help understand these scientific advances?

Take, for example, the experience of Loretta. More than thirty years ago she came down with a devastating case of rheumatic fever, a form of strep infection that was much deadlier in those days.

Loretta's physician prescribed penicillin for her. She spent at least two weeks with an intense fever without getting any better.

Although she had not had a cardiac arrest or was moved to the hospital, she had an experience after two weeks of being very sick that could only be described as an NDE.

Though we do not know if she died clinically, we do know from her medical records that she was extremely ill and under great stress. We also know that she reported a "strange experience" at the time. And she says it was her experience with the light that led to her rapid recovery shortly after having this NDE.

What follows in is Loretta's experience of healing in her own words.

"OH MY GOODNESS, I'M DEAD!"

"I had scarlet fever and I was at home. My pediatrician wanted me kept on the davenport in the living room where everyone would pass by me all the time and keep an eye on me.

"I was very sick and had been for quite awhile. I got so bad that my family had to pick me up and carry me around. I had no energy and felt as if my physical strength was leaving me. I remember thinking I was going to die because my physical energy was just sort of draining away.

"Finally one day I remember trying to hang on to my strength and feeling it slip away like I was falling off a cliff. I had the distinct feeling that I was dying.

"The next thing I knew I was in a tunnel and it was completely black. Of course at that time I was in a black void and I didn't realize it was a tunnel. Then I seemed to look around and I saw this light. I didn't have any sense of fear or fright. I did have a sense that I was flowing toward the light. I also had a feeling that I didn't have a body but that I was a complete being.

"It was then that I had the sense of being above the ceiling, above the front windows, above the bookcase. I could look down and see my mother in the dining room and my sister standing there with her. I could see them right through the walls. I could also see my body there on the couch. I wasn't afraid, but I remember thinking, 'oh my goodness, I'm dead!'

"Even though I was looking down at everything, I started really being aware of the light. I did not see God, but I felt God. I didn't hear any voices, I didn't see anyone I knew from the past. I didn't see any flowers or anything—just the light. It was as if I was a phantom body. I felt God surround me and embrace me in a way that there was no division between the inside and the outside of my skin. I felt as though the light and love was permeating me. It was all through me, completely. I felt infinite contentment, peace and love. I have never forgotten that feeling. From that moment on I have had no fear of death at all.

"I started watching my sister. She came into the living room and stood looking at me. She walked by the coffee table to the davenport and looked at me very closely.

"I looked down at myself and noticed that my skin was so ivory that it was translucent. It wasn't white or gray, it was ivory with a green tinge underneath it.

"My sister looked at me for a moment and then went back into the dining room. She walked over to the buffet and took out the camera. At that time my mother looked up from what she was doing and watched my sister. There was a wall between them and my body, but I could see all of this going on because I wasn't in my body.

"I watched as my sister put the camera to her face and took a picture. At that time a thought came into my mind: 'You have to go back into your body and finish your life.' "

Loretta's scarlet fever was gone within the next two days. The doctor was surprised at the rapid recovery. So was Loretta's mother, who said she had been very near death. "All of us, including the doctor, thought there was a good chance you wouldn't make it," she said. About a week later Loretta told her mother about the experience. She had a strong feeling that it had led to her rapid healing.

MINIMAL HEALING

Did it? I think it triggered an electromagnetic charge that stimulated her body's immune system. Dr. Becker, the bioelectric researcher, calls this type of healing one of *minimal energy*, in that it relies on the energy generated by the body with no external input. For instance, people who just think about lowering their heart rate or blood pressure can usually do it. This is called *biofeedback*, and is an example of a mental process affecting the physical body. I am willing to go so far as to say that in many ways healings that happen through NDEs are a form of the same thing.

Remember: the human body is a machine driven by energy. When that energy changes, so does the machine.

I have explained how electrical charges to the right temporal lobe can cause positive personality changes. Of course, the entire book is based upon a study that explores the many ways in which people who have near-death experiences are different from those who do not. Let me give you an example of one person who was changed abruptly by her NDE so you can see how quickly such a transformation can occur. I have begun to consider NDEs as an electrical charge similar to a mild electroshock.

ANNIE'S TRANSFORMATION

Annie was a very depressed teenager. By the age of sixteen she had experimented with drugs, alcohol, boys, and all the other teenage vices. When her boyfriend announced at a party that he was leaving her for another girl, Annie decided to kill herself. Her mother had committed suicide a few years before. As Annie told it, "I just decided to emulate my mother." She picks up the story from there:

"I decided to kill myself just the way my mother had. I took a handful of barbiturates and swallowed them with vodka, lots of it. I gulped down as much vodka as I could and went back out to the living room where the party was going on.

"I just sat on the couch and didn't say anything. I could feel the mixture coming over me and I began to doze off. The funny thing was that nobody noticed since most of my friends were a little bit high themselves.

"If I had lain back, I would have fallen asleep and died and nobody would have noticed. But instead I was sitting forward when I passed out and just fell facedown onto the floor.

"A bunch of people panicked. A couple of the boys carried me to the bathroom and one of my girlfriends put her finger in my throat and made me throw up in the bathtub. No one wanted to call the police so they decided to keep me awake and give me a shower. They turned on the shower and kept talking to me.

"It took me awhile to realize that I was out of my body and floating up by the ceiling. I wasn't alone. There was someone else there, a Guardian Angel or something. We were both made of light. I felt three-dimensional and I seemed to be made of something that wasn't solid, maybe gelatin.

"I remember feeling love and peace and also feeling as though I had escaped from all the tension and frustration in my life. I felt kind of enveloped by light. It was a wonderful feeling.

"I was very close to my Guardian Angel at this point. I could no longer see my body or anything earthly. I just was there with the angel. The angel didn't speak, but it communicated. I was shown the beauty of my body and of every body. I was told that my body was a gift and I was supposed to take care of it, not kill it. After hearing this, I felt very, very ashamed of what I had done and hoped that I would live. I began to beg the light for life. The feeling that came back was the strongest feeling of love I have ever experienced, even more than the feeling of love I have for my own children.

"My friends had taken me to a hospital, because the next thing I remember was waking up in an emergency room."

Annie says the experience changed her attitude immediately, as it does with most NDEers. She told her boyfriend to beat it, she stopped drinking and drugging and as a result developed a new set of friends.

I don't want to give the impression that the experience made her a goodie two-shoes, but it certainly changed her attitude for the better. She no longer dwelled upon her mother's suicide. Instead of thinking of life as a series of trials, she found it a pleasure to behold.

The transformation has been a long-term one for Annie. Her near-death experience happened more than twenty years ago. Now she is happily married with four sons. "Immediately after the experience I felt as though I had been given a mission in life, like I was born to accomplish something," says Annie. "The experience gave me an inner energy that has never left me."

Her case and so many like it are a strong indication that this form of electroshock therapy occurs. The long-term effects of the NDE are a testament to its power to make significant changes in personality. I want to point out that these changes in personality cannot take place without significant changes in brain physiology. As many researchers have pointed out, changes in personality—especially long-term changes—are almost always accompanied by changes in the actual makeup of the brain.

EXPLAIN THE PARANORMAL

This electromagnetic theory provides a solid explanation for telepathic communications and the seeing of apparitions at the point of death. In fact, it has been theorized that these two types of experience represent nothing more than a person's ability to sense another person's electrical field. This explains why telepathy usually involves the vague perceptions of feelings, emotions, or indistinct images as opposed to the direct reading of thoughts on a literal level. Since the right temporal lobe is the nonverbal portion of the brain, these perceptions are interpreted in a nonverbal way.

Based upon our research and observations, I feel that NDEers become sensitized to the world around them in a way that is entirely unique.

Let me give one such example. I shall call this woman Allison. She had a near-death experience more than ten years ago that led to a great change in her personality. She had a few instances in which she was able to tell what people were going to say before they said it, but, beyond that, there was nothing extraordinary about her psychic powers.

About ten years later, she was able to see her son leave his body at the point of death. I do not know that there is any relationship between the NDE she had and her ability to see her son's essence leaving his body. In theory, I think she became sensitized as a result of the NDE and actually saw her son's light shout.

First here is Allison's NDE:

"In 1980 I had cancer surgery and apparently had a reaction from the anesthetic. While I was in the recovery room, I 'left' and zoomed toward a brilliant and indescribable light. A man was with me who was very gentle. He took me into the light where I experienced a kind of love that I have never been able to explain.

"It was a wonderful experience, but I suddenly had the feeling that I was leaving this world, that I was going to die. I didn't want to go! I had two children and I didn't know what would happen to them if I wasn't around.

"As though he could read my mind, the man with me laughed and said: 'You aren't dying. You still have not done what you are supposed to do.'

"Something drew me back the way we had come. Then I regained consciousness. My nurse was on the phone when I opened my eyes and she looked very relieved. 'I thought I had lost you,' she said.

More than ten years later she found herself in the same hospital standing watch over her son who had a septic infection of his blood as a result of diabetes. He was in the intensive care unit when he suffered what would prove to be a fatal cardiac arrest.

Once again she tells the story:

"I was hysterical. Doctors ran into the room and I was ushered out while the doctors worked over his body. I could watch through glass windows in the hall as they did their work. I was crying because I expected the worst.

"Suddenly I saw him fly right out of his body! I could see this misty wisp go right up. He moved around near the ceiling for a few seconds and then he just disappeared!

"One of the doctors came out and told me that they had gotten him back but I knew they hadn't. I told him that I had just seen my boy leave his body and the doctor asked if I would like to sit down. A few moments later another doctor came out and announced that he had died."

There are many cases of people seeing an essence leave a dying person's body. I think one of the ways in which near-death experiencers are changed is in their ability to see or otherwise sense the electromagnetic forces of other people and things.

Although they can't sense this electromagnetism on a consistent basis, I do feel they can experience it much more frequently than can non-NDEers. As Dr. Andrew Deak said: "Our brain is like a transmission with five hundred gears and we only know four of them. Perhaps the NDE introduces us to a few more of them."

A UNIFYING THEORY

The idea that the near-death experience changes a person's electromagnetic force field greatly clarifies a number of the changes that take place in NDEers. Spontaneous healings, personality transformation, telepathy, and out-of-body experiences are all paranormal experiences that become normal when viewed in this context. All of these events have been linked to the right temporal lobe by my previous research and that of many other medical scientists.

Dr. Wilder Penfield, the father of modern neuroscience, found that stimulating the temporal lobe of some of his patients during brain surgery would create the vivid sensation of leaving their bodies. Others, like Dr. Vernon Neppe, the preeminent expert on déjà vu, have found that recall of past events is linked to the temporal lobe.

I realize that this concept—on the surface at least—seems to diminish the religious or mystical experience. Most people have been content to let mystical experiences be mysterious ones, too. Still, I do not think that explaining a process as marvelous as the near-death experience and localizing it within the brain ruins the experience. After all, we are human. All human experiences are supposed to be processed and interpreted someplace in the human body.

A verse from the Bible sums up my feelings about this subject very nicely. It is also interesting in that it sums up the thinking of scientists like Stephen Hawking:

". . . God made all things, not one thing in all creation was made without him. The Word was the source of life, and this life brought light to mankind. The light shines in the darkness and the darkness has never put it out. The Word was in the world, and though God made the world through him, yet the world did not recognize him."

7

The Transformations Artifacts

"Science rests on a tripod whose legs are hypothesis, observation and faith."

—*Timothy Ferris*

All good scientific studies lead to more questions than answers. The Transformations study was no different. Although we proudly went where no researchers have yet gone with our examination of near-death experiences, we also opened the door on many other areas that will have to be researched in the future. We call these areas artifacts, because they emerge unexpectedly and are not examined as part of the study.

I mention them in my scientific papers so other researchers can pursue them in future projects. These artifacts, or unexpected findings, can often lead to the most important insights and understandings.

For example, a Boston pathologist in the 1920s was studying the long-term effects of alcohol on the muscle fibers of the heart. While examining the hearts of deceased alcoholics he noticed something strange: As alcoholics waste away from drink, the fat and cholesterol that blocked their arteries sometimes disappears, leaving scar tissue as a reminder that it was there. Ironically, blockages in arteries became smaller as the alcoholics became sicker.

This artifact led some researchers to pursue regression studies, or ways in which heart disease can be reversed.

There are some such puzzling artifacts in the Transformations study. These are pleasant surprises that occur at a statistically significant rate. I am including them in this book in hope that some other researchers might become fascinated by them and launch a project of their own. I also have my opinion on their cause and effect, which I am also happy to share.

As you will see, there is much that is unknown about the near-death experiences which remains to be researched.

THE TRANSFORMING LIGHT

The Transformations study neatly documents the fact that people who have near-death experiences are changed for life. Those changes are most profound in the NDEers who have experiences of light. This was true whether they had a vivid and powerful memory of a flower-filled heaven bursting with light, or just a brief and fleeting memory of seeing the light.

We also found that people who have a mystical experience of light—whether in a lucid dream or simply tripping into an altered state, *without being near death*—are just as transformed as those who have a near-death experience.

Most of these people experience the mystical light as the result of a life-threatening situation, but some have "seen the light" while driving cars, jogging, watching television, or taking walks in the forest. These are ordinary people. Yet they have had the same experiences as great mystics and religious leaders.

Let me give you an example of one such experience. I shall call this woman Jane. She was trying to fall asleep one night after a particularly rough day. Her husband was asleep next to her. She was lying there with her thoughts when suddenly she saw a terrible face, "like an evil ET," that was "glowing with a brownish-green glow."

"I tried to tell my husband what I was seeing but he couldn't hear me. Suddenly that face faded and a beautiful light filled the room. A Being appeared, glowing white and beautiful. I suddenly seemed to get a history review, towns and people and buildings appeared before me. I saw people from the olden days with robes and sandals. There was a war going on between good and evil. The evil face came into view from time to time, but the Being of Light was stronger.

"The last thing I saw was Jesus beckoning to me, with Light shooting out of his body. I felt he was welcoming me. I wanted to get up and tried, but then I saw my feet withdraw into my body. Then it all floated down the hall and disappeared."

This experience had elements of a near-death experience, such as seeing a glowing being and a beautiful light. Yet this woman was in no way near death. As a result of this experience she now describes the afterlife as "total freedom and peace of mind." She took this experience as being proof of an afterlife and although she is not religious, she is very spiritual and has explored many different religions.

She, like all the people in this group which we labeled "Experience of Light—No Near Death," tested extremely low on death anxiety. She also scored very high on the Greyson Near-Death Experience Validity Scale, the test all study participants were given to validate whether or not they had a real NDE. All the people in this group scored as high as NDEers in validity of experience.

"LIKE HAVING TWO SETS OF EYES"

Here is another example from this group. I'll call this man Jim. He had what some researchers call a "Fear Death Experience," because his NDE occurred when he was in a frightening situation but was not technically near death.

This experience of light happened to Jim when he was a high school student in California. On a summer day while staying at his parent's beach house, he decided to go open water diving. He and a friend donned their diving gear and swam straight out into the ocean, about three hundred yards offshore. They dove down into the murky water until their tanks were empty and then began the long swim back to shore.

Being novice divers they forgot to check tide tables. Soon they realized that the tide was going out and they were being slowly pushed out toward sea. In no time they were separated and struggling for shore. That was when Jim left his body and saw the light:

"I was feeling tired and scared as I kicked for shore. I was using my snorkel and swimming with my face in the water and I looked up to see where I was. When I realized I was farther away from the shore I became really frightened and began kicking harder.

"All of a sudden I was up in the air looking down at myself swimming. It was literally like having two sets of eyes connected to the same brain.

"My first reaction was, *how is this happening?* I was about three feet above myself and a little behind. I could see the shoreline and where I was headed. I could also look down in the water and see what was going on down there. There was no distortion of anything and I could see in a panoramic way, about 270 degrees.

"Then I became engulfed in a fluffy, bright light. It had substance like a cloud and was all around me. I felt good in it and even a little bit revived.

"Then—pop—I was back in my body. I think the whole experience lasted about a minute."

Jim was not near death, he was in "fear death," which means he was in a life-threatening situation. Yet despite not having been technically near death, he has the same psychological profile as those in the near-death experience group. His death anxiety is extremely low and his zest for life index puts him solidly in line with NDEers. Also he tests very high on the NDE validity scale.

A CIRCUIT BOARD RESPONSE

What does it mean that some people have these experiences of light without being near death? Does it make them less real? Does it make the experiences mere fantasies? Does it cheapen the belief that these somehow open spiritual realms not ordinarily open to us? In short, does it make the experience of light just psychological?

I say emphatically no. In research I have documented a spot in the brain that functions as the circuit board of mysticism. It is in this spot, located above the right ear in an area known as the temporal lobe, that the symptoms of the near-death experience take place. These are most commonly triggered by death or near death. I have come to believe that other events can trigger this circuit board as well. Fear can set it off, intense stress, even being in a state of drowsy half sleep.

The transformative part of the experience is seeing the light. If a person has a paranormal experience such as leaving their body but it is *not* accompanied by the light, then the experience is not usually transformative. If the light is experienced then there is a transformation. The transformative powers are in the light. That is what our research tells us.

I think that localizing the experience to a spot in the brain gives it substance. People who have these experiences of light—whether near death or not—gain comfort knowing that there is an area of the brain coded for this experience. Likewise, scientists will be more interested in studying NDEs and other paranormal occurrences if they know there is a place in the brain where they are supposed to take place. Knowing where the cir-

cuit boards of mysticism are gives researchers something real to work with.

GUARDIANS AND GHOSTS

A large percentage of near-death experiencers in my
study had encounters with deceased people in the
course of their NDE. That means that they saw a dead
relative or a person whom they knew was dead. Also,
many NDEers meet guardian angels in the course of
their near-death experience. These guardians function as
guides or companions to the person as they travel up the
tunnel on their journey to the light.

The guardian angels are usually experienced only
during the NDE. However, a large number of people in
the Transformations study retain contact with the guardian angel even after having their near-death experience.
Many are able to communicate with this angel in their
daily lives, receiving soothing advice during periods of
emotional or physical stress.

I was surprised to find that about 12 percent of the
people in the Transformations study have regular contact with the guardian angels that they saw during their
NDEs.

By the same token, over 10 percent of near-death experiencers report seeing ghosts or other apparitions after
their NDEs. These may include dead relatives or even
people they have never seen before.

Let me give some examples of each and then I'll
comment on this phenomenon.

GUARDIAN ANGELS

David, the bestselling author mentioned in chapter one, is one of the more interesting examples of someone who has maintained a lifelong relationship with a so-called guardian angel.

He first encountered a guardian angel during his bout with hepatitis as a child. The angel appeared to him as a fourth person in the room, standing behind his mother, father, and the doctor who were all at his bedside. He had an out-of-body experience in which he stood with the angel for a brief period of time. Then he returned to his body.

The guardian angel has been with him since then, although he does not see her anymore. Instead he senses her presence, "like someone standing in the room with me," he says. Growing up she kept him company when he was alone and even helped him with his homework. As an adult she helps with his writing. He can tell when she takes over because he no longer feels in control.

"It happens to me a lot on the stuff I write. I wrote something last night and I don't know where the hell it comes from.

"My wife can go through my manuscripts with a red pen and circle the stuff that doesn't look like my own. And I don't know where it comes from. It's the most powerful imagery in the world.

"But where am I when this stuff is coming out? I'm not sitting in the chair. I'm gone. When I'm done I frequently feel like I'm going to faint. I need to get a cup of coffee or talk my wife into giving me a back rub. Then I sit down and read my stuff and it's the first time I've read it. I don't know where it's coming from. It happens with such frequency that I feel like I'm a fraud. I don't feel like it's coming from me and it leads to some spooky times.

"I know my fingers are moving and I know words are appearing on the screen, but it's as though they aren't coming out of my head. And I have a very strange, detached feeling. I'll get up and take a break and then read the work and it's as though someone came through the window and stuck it on my computer."

I wish I could quote from some of the work that David is talking about. The imagery is especially powerful, the dialogue gripping. However he wants to remain anonymous, citing the belief that most people would think it peculiar if they thought they were reading the work of a guardian angel.

"I SAW A LITTLE GIRL FLOATING"

A more visual representation of a guardian angel comes from a boy we shall call Russ. He was four years old when he was accidentally pushed from a tree house by some of his friends. It was during the fall that he encountered the angel.

"I looked up and suddenly I was falling, but it felt more like I was floating. I heard a voice tell me not to be scared, but to hold very still and to look up and not move my neck. It said that it would hurt but I would still be okay.

"I saw a little girl floating in the air next to me. She was all bright, but it didn't hurt my eyes to look at her.

"I did what I was told and landed hard and broke my collarbone.

"When I got to the doctor, I heard him tell my mother that if my head had been turned to the left or the right, I would have snapped my neck. I did just what the little girl told me to do and walked away okay."

BATTLEFIELD ANGEL

Here is another story to give you an idea of the breadth of guardian angel experiences and the variety of people who have them. This happened to a businessman named Richard, who had joined the Marines at the age of seventeen to "get in on the action" of battle in Vietnam.

During a firefight with the enemy, Richard was wounded several times while many of those around him were killed. Here's how he tells the story:

"I was down and in a lot of pain. I looked up to heaven and begged God to let me die like my friends around me. All of a sudden I felt no pain at all. I just went above myself and saw myself with a broken ankle and bleeding wounds all over my body. I felt no pain.

"Then all around me came this beautiful shining light. That's all, a beautiful shining light and no pain."

Richard does not consider himself to be religious or spiritual. Yet to this day, when undergoing pain or severe stress, a glimmer of the light appears to him, and with it comes a "joyous peace."

GHOSTS

A typical ghost sighting comes from Janice, who had a near-death experience in the course of back surgery. She felt as though she had rolled into a ball and was hurtling through a pipe toward a bright light. She did have the experience of being engulfed by the light, but that was the sum total of her NDE.

She has had several verifiable psychic experiences and sightings of apparitions. Here are two of them:

"My father had to have a total hip replacement when he was very old. It was a difficult surgery and one that he didn't recover from. After about a week in the hospital, he died of a blood clot that moved into his heart and killed him.

"Several weeks after his funeral I woke up early in the morning to see my father standing next to the bed. I got up and walked with him to the living room. He was walking fine, without a limp. All he said was that he had tuberculosis of the bone and he wanted us to know.

"I don't know why it was important that we know, but when I checked with his doctor he confirmed that the bone was filled with TB."

Here is another one:

"In college a bunch of us girls traveled to another college to watch our basketball teams play. We stayed in an old house near the campus.

"In the afternoon I was in a little sitting room reading when I saw a man at the top of the stairs. He was wearing a top hat and tails and was looking down at me.

"It was odd but not really frightening. I just sat there and looked up at him until he disappeared. Then I asked the owner of the house who that man was. The only possible identity he could come up with was that he was the former mayor of the town who had once lived in the house."

A KNOCK AT THE DOOR

Here is another report of an apparition from a woman named Susan, who has had nearly a dozen verifiable psychic experiences and three reported ghost sightings.

"My grandmother had been dead for several years when this happened. I think it was strange, but I can honestly say that I wasn't frightened, just puzzled.

"There was a knock at my door one night. I thought it was one of the neighbors or something so I just opened up. Standing there was my grandmother!

"She walked into the room, walked once around it and walked back out. That was it! To this day I don't understand it but it doesn't scare me."

CONNECTION TO THE DIVINE

"Saw grandfather in the room with me shortly before he died."

"I saw my grandmother walk by and heard her footsteps. I found out later that she had died."

"When my best friend died he stood in front of me in my room. I didn't know he had died and I was scared. When he started to speak I ran from the room."

The Transformations study was full of just such encounters with the dead. Many of these "events" have cryptic elements to them, like the father who returned to say he had TB in his bone. The information seemed to have no value. Yet it was something no one in the family knew until the daughter saw her father as a ghost.

Just what do these guardian and ghost experiences mean?

I think such experiences can be considered a person's link with the spiritual, a sort of connection to the good things they saw in the bright light. It may even be a sort of continuation of the light experience itself.

Part of this comes down to the fact that the right hemisphere of the brain is sensitized by the NDE. It is the right temporal lobe, according to brain researchers, that has its own consciousness and communicates with pictures and holographic images.

I also think that this area of the brain is capable of responding to electromagnetic energy and the vibes, if you will, of other people. As you know from chapter six, this increased sensitivity could be why NDEers have far more psychic experiences from the rest of the population. Since ghosts are explained by some theorists as being nothing more than a dead person's electromagnetic energy, this theory could also explain why NDEers see them. Increased electromagnetic sensitivity could nicely explain such phenomena as dowsing, remote viewing, even acupuncture.

Does this theory demystify these spiritual experiences by localizing them in the brain? Not as far as I'm concerned. Just as the practice of medicine changes with the advent of new technology, so must our spiritual beliefs be reevaluated with new scientific findings.

Guardians and ghosts are certainly a link to the light within us. But the source of that light is still a mystery.

CAN NEAR-DEATH EXPERIENCES BE SHARED?

I have encountered so many shared near-death experiences that the subject almost deserves its own chapter.

I define a shared NDE as one in which someone experiences another person's death. Not physically, mind you. We are talking about experiencing it through some form of clairvoyance.

Let me give you an example:

I received a phone call one day from a very upset mother who wanted to know if it was possible to *witness* a near-death experience. Her seventeen-year-old son, Shane, had recently died in a traffic accident. He was riding his bicycle and was struck by a truck. Thrown through the air, he suffered massive head injuries.

His parents were called to the hospital where he had been taken. They found their son brain dead and being kept alive by life-support machines. He died several hours later.

They went home to break the news to their fifteen-year-old daughter who was deaf. She was not even aware that her brother was dead.

When they went into the house, they were surprised to find her in a trance but conscious. She was talking to someone. She said it was her brother. The girl said she had been taking a nap after school when she could suddenly see and hear her brother. She said she was awake and able to look around her room, but at the same time she was in another world. She was still in that other world when her distraught parents came in the door.

She described the accident. She could see her brother flying through the air and knew without being told that he was really dead at the scene. Her brother seemed to be calling her, although he was not speaking in words. "I've got to show you something really cool," he communicated.

The two of them rose in the air, high above the scene of the accident. Her brother had apparently been there before because he said to her, "Wait until you see what's next!"

Cheryl, the deaf sister, says that they then went to heaven. While in heaven she met relatives who had died but she could still see her mother standing there in the living room and was able to see her late brother. She was able to speak, so her family was able to hear what she thought Shane was saying to her. At one point he started teasing his sister, saying, "I know something you don't know," over and over again. Finally he told her that their aunt was pregnant with a boy, a fact unknown to the family at the time.

This event was witnessed by three family members, all of whom are normal healthy adults who have no reason to invent such a story and many reasons not to publicize it. The mother discusses it freely, believing it's proof that her son survived bodily death. Her husband, one of the eyewitnesses, refuses to discuss the incident.

STRONG EVIDENCE, NOT PROOF

I believe Cheryl's story because I have heard many like it. I have documented several stories just like this one, from people who feel that they have witnessed someone else's death. For me these stories have significant meaning. Not *scientific* meaning. No, Cheryl's story is not scientific proof of anything. Science requires a hypothesis which can then be used to explain experimentally derived facts as well as predict the outcome of future experiments. Science requires a research design which is reproducible, one that can occur over and over, again and again, given a certain set of conditions. The experiment must then be able to be repeated by other scientists who achieve the same results.

So Cheryl's story and others like it are not scientific proof of anything. I find them interesting because, like near-death experiences, these are paranormal experiences that happen to normal people.

I am always careful about how I approach these stories. For instance I tend to discount any story that I don't hear directly from the source. If someone says, "I have a friend who knew somebody who . . ." I know it is most likely a sort of modern folktale. Modern folktales are stories told over and over as though they were true. You are certainly familiar with some of the most common of them: the vanishing hitchhiker, the Kentucky fried rat, even Bigfoot. These are stories that are passed on, yet have no basis in fact.

Dr. Jan Brunwald has spent his life researching such legends yet has been unable to find objective evidence that these events and hundreds like them ever took place. All he has found is word of mouth, someone saying "I have a friend who who knew somebody who . . ."

I insist upon talking to the people who had the experiences. I meticulously document these cases, sometimes even audio- or videotaping my interview with the person. Dr. Ian Stevenson, a noted researcher from the University of Virginia, feels that the most important new paranormal research will come from documented cases of paranormal events. Stevenson says that this kind of evidence from ordinary people who are obviously sincere and telling the truth may well be the best direct evidence that we have available.

CAREFUL DOCUMENTATION

I documented that Shane was in fact a patient who had died in a traffic accident at the hospital. I interviewed each of the people who witnessed Cheryl's experience. I spoke with character witnesses who verified that, yes, this was a typical family. My conclusion after all this documentation was that this girl had indeed shared her brother's death experience.

I also believe, after examining so many of these shared experiences, that they provide excellent evidence that the light, and much else that is seen by near-death experiencers, originates from outside the body. Somehow another person is able to experience what a dying person is experiencing.

Of course this implies that the near-death experience (or in some cases, the *dying* experience) can be telepathically shared. This is not so far-fetched as it may seem. Rupert Sheldrake, a Ph.D. biologist and Fellow of the Royal Society in England, believes that our temporal lobes may act as antennae to interact with energy fields outside of our bodies. This is one possible explanation for telepathy (being able to communicate with no words or visual cues) and, of course, for the sharing of NDEs and other paranormal experiences.

Sheldrake claims that the force field surrounding all living organisms is a form of species memory that exists outside the organism's body which allows it to determine its form. Sheldrake calls this "morphic resonance," in which animals learn from each other and grow based upon a species' pooled memory.

Although memory is stored within the human brain, Sheldrake thinks it may also exist outside the body in these "morphogenic force fields" and may be picked up like radio waves by the temporal lobes of other people.

Perhaps this is an explanation for a variety of paranormal experiences such as the telepathy that exists between couples who have been married for many years or between twins. It could certainly explain the sharing of a near-death or death experience.

This is just one of the theories that must be examined in the future.

FROM OTHER SOURCES

There are many examples of these shared experiences in both popular and medical literature. Here are some:

- United Press International reported on May 30, 1970, that Romer Troxell was driving from his home in Pennsylvania to Portage, Indiana, where he had the unhappy task of identifying his murdered son's mortal remains. From the moment he entered the city, he felt his son's voice speaking to him. The voice gave him driving instructions, which he followed to Gary, Indiana.

There, he spotted his son's car being driven down a back street. He forced the car off the road and stayed with the driver while a relative who had made the trip with him called the police.

The man in the car was later convicted of the murder of Troxell's son.

- In the late 1800s and early 1900s, two British intellectuals by the names of F.W.H. Meyers and Edmund Gurney collected hundreds of stories of the paranormal, many of them shared experiences.

In one typical case from 1863, a Mr. Conley went to Dubuque, Iowa, for medical treatment and died. His son was notified by telegraph and went to Dubuque to bring back the body. They returned with the body and most of his clothing, leaving some of it in Dubuque.

After coming home, Elizabeth Conley, the dead man's daughter, claimed she had a vision in which her father returned and told her to get the money out of his undershirt.

The brother returned to Dubuque and found thirty dollars wrapped in the undershirt.

- The television program "Unsolved Mysteries" broadcast the story of a young respiratory therapist in Dallas who was found murdered in her apartment. There were no suspects and no clues until another respiratory therapist at the same hospital began having a dream. In that dream the murdered therapist came to her and said: "I have been murdered by Edward Copina," an orderly who worked at the same hospital.

She awoke in a fright and told her husband, who

was a physician at the same hospital. They dismissed the event as a nightmare.

And yet the dream happened again. And then a third time in which the frightened physician watched as his wife seemed to be possessed by the dead woman's spirit. "Why haven't you gone to the police?" the physician was asked by his seemingly possessed wife.

"Because we have no evidence. They will ignore us!"

"The evidence is in the jewelry," said the wife. "He took some of my jewelry."

The couple went to the police and told them what had happened. Rather than reject their testimony, the policy questioned the orderly and he admitted to the murder. Later it was discovered that his girlfriend was wearing the dead woman's jewelry.

SOMETIMES NO COMFORT

I will candidly admit that these stories almost always defy rational belief. Sometimes these shared experiences do not solve any sort of family crisis. If anything, they add to the confusion of the moment. On top of dealing with the loss or near loss of a loved one, they must also try to explain an experience that does not fit into their view of what life is all about.

Let me give you an example of one such experience that proved to be of no comfort for the woman who had it.

We will call this woman Donna. She and her husband were on their honeymoon in Hawaii when she had a very vivid dream that her brother on the mainland had been killed.

In the dream, she found herself hovering over her brother's hospital bed. She tried to communicate with him, but was unable to get him to open his eyes. After hovering there for several seconds, she could hear her brother say that he was going to die.

"He just looked like he was sleeping," she said. "I knew he had massive head injuries, but he didn't look bad."

Early the next morning she told her husband about the dream but he dismissed it as being caused by a late dinner. They left for the mainland right after breakfast.

At their hometown airport they happened to meet her sister. They found out from her that their brother had been struck by a car and died of massive brain injury after three days in intensive care.

Having this experience was no comfort for Donna. For one thing, she did not like having a premonition of any kind. For another, it gave both her and her husband deep feelings of guilt. As he said, "I want to make my decisions based on fact. So I wouldn't let her call home. I said, 'If anything is really wrong they would call us.' "

Donna's mother had her own disturbing interpretation of her daughter's shared experience. She thought Satan was sending those dreams. Donna feels very strongly the other way. She thinks they were heaven-sent. "I think God wanted me to be the strong one for the family so he told me in a special way."

Still this was not a comforting experience for Donna or anyone else in her family. To this day her experience is a source of stress for the family as it struggles to explain what seems to be unexplainable.

A SHARED DREAM

Here is another story from the Midwest that illustrates the many dilemmas in understanding these shared experiences.

This involves a mother whose nine-year-old daughter was critically ill with leukemia. On this particular night she slept with her daughter as she frequently did during her illness.

She awoke the next morning to describe an incredible dream to her husband. She went through a long tunnel with her daughter. At the end of the tunnel was a beautiful place filled with colors and the sound of music. There were little children and babies everywhere and a lighted figure that she described as Christ. He spoke to her. He said that it was not her daughter's time to die and that she would have to wait "there on earth" a while longer. He further said that when the time came, the mother would follow shortly thereafter, which was yet to happen as of publication.

Within an hour the daughter described the same dream to her father. She, too, described going through the long tunnel and seeing a room filled with colors and music. And she spoke to Jesus who said the same thing to her that she had to the mother.

There is irony in this shared experience. Where the mother found great comfort in the experience, the daughter gained no comfort from it at all. It frightened and angered her and she remained that way until she died a few months later.

She never experienced the peace and calm that many do before dying and she did not lose her fear of death as a result of the dream. The father also had a hard time coming to terms with this experience. For a while he thought his wife had gone mad. When he realized the illogic of that, he became angry that his daughter had been allowed to die, but he was also mad because he was not privileged enough to have the experience along with his wife and daughter.

So here we have a shared experience that comforts the mother, brings no comfort to the sick child, and alienates the father.

This brings up a point that applies to studying these shared visions: Simply having a death-related vision is not a panacea for all issues related to death and dying.

RIPE FIELD FOR STUDY

I am anxious to examine these shared experiences more closely. It is important to document these cases to the best of our abilities. Proving these experiences really happened is one of the largest pieces to the puzzle we call paranormal research.

I also think that the level of proof we are required to present is irrationally high. Most of our modern medical and scientific advances are based on scientific data far *less* documented than the eyewitness and independently verified stories we hear in our research. For example, most of our infant feeding practices are based on statistically suspect or anecdotal studies. Most people believe in the existence of infant colic, yet it is difficult to find any consensus in the medical literature on what it is and how to treat it. Even the value of having a low serum cholesterol, something almost completely accepted by the public, is the subject of debate in scientific circles.

Despite the controversy, we build guidelines to live by from these accepted "facts." Why? Simply because the principles we follow work most of the time and don't really change our world view. We feed babies a certain way, treat them for something we can only loosely define as colic, and keep our cholesterol levels low even if the why is not scientifically nailed down. We do this because, frankly, these rules do not interfere too much with our lives.

Since there is so much documentation to back up these shared experiences, why are they and other spiritual experiences not generally accepted as being true? I think the answer is quite simple. Believing in them would radically change our world view, challenging everything from natural laws to spiritual beliefs.

SIGHTING NOT BELIEVED

A poignant example of this is offered by Carol Staudacher, a California psychologist and grief counselor. In her book *Beyond Grief* she offers some fine examples of shared experiences from her own practice.

In one of the stories, a woman sees her deceased husband in a doorway, wearing a white bathrobe. This woman's mother-in-law was also in the room with her. She said nothing and did not act as if anything was out of the ordinary. Yet later, this woman learns that her mother-in-law had seen the same vision, with the same bathrobe.

Here is the dilemma: The two women see the same

vision, yet they cannot speak of it to each other. Each discusses it privately and learns through the grapevine of the other's experience, which at the very least was a telepathically shared hallucination or perhaps a shared memory.

What they saw was not such a big deal. The fact that they both saw the same thing at the same time was what is remarkable about this experience.

ARE NEONATAL NDES POSSIBLE?

A surprise finding of the Transformations study is that infants may be able to experience NDEs. I was able to document several in the study, with the youngest being four months of age.

Most of these were extremely simple, usually involving memories of the bright light or flight up the tunnel. Here is a typical example, this from a man who almost died at the age of four months:

"All I remember is seeing a very bright light all around me and having an intense feeling of love."

Here is an *atypical* example, this from a teenager named Mark who nearly died at the age of nine months:

"I saw nurses and doctors standing over me trying to wake me up. I flew out of the room and [went to the waiting room, where I] saw Grandpa and Grandma crying and holding each other. I think they thought I was going to die."

Later he reported crawling up a long, dark tunnel toward a bright light. At the end of the tunnel he found a "bright place" and "ran through fields with God."

God asked him if he wanted to go "back home." Mark said "no" but he was sent back anyway.

I ran across one of these baby NDEs while researching *Closer to the Light* and did not really expect to find many more. I did find several more while doing the Transformations study, including one person who claimed to have had an NDE *prenatally!*

I know this sounds incredible, and no one is more surprised than I am. I, like most of my colleagues in pediatrics, have been trained to believe that long-term memory is not something of which infants are capable. More and more research is piling up to show that infants have the ability to be cognizant of their surroundings and to memorize events.

BETTER MEMORY THAN ONCE THOUGHT

For example, American psychiatrist Nandor Fodor described dozens of his patients in the forties and fifties who remembered specific traumatic events of their birth. Some even mentioned prenatal memories such as hearing the sound of firecrackers or train whistles. He even collected cases suggesting telepathy between mother and infant. I have personally heard such cases as well.

David Cheek, a San Francisco obstetrician, has collected a number of stories documenting birth memories. One of the more striking ones involves a compulsive overachiever in his fifties, who had a dramatic resolution of his anxiety and lack of self-worth when he remembered hearing the obstetrician at his own birth tell a nurse, "Don't waste too much time on this one. I don't think he's worth saving." This man was born two and a half months early and at three-and-one-half pounds, his doctor thought he was going to die.

David Chamberlain, a respected psychologist, has an interesting protocol with which to study birth memory. He examined ten mother/child pairs in which the children ranged in age from nine to twenty-three years of age. The children had no conscious memory of their births, and their mothers had not discussed the specifics of their births in any way.

He then hypnotized the children and regressed them back to their births, recording their birth memories. He recorded such details as the time of day, people present, instruments used, type of delivery (head or feet first), sequence of receiving feedings or bottles, appearance and disappearance of fathers, and being moved from room to room. This memory was compared with the details of the birth provided by the mothers.

On the average, the mother/child pairs described fourteen details which precisely matched. The best pair had twenty-four specific details match and no contradictions. The worst case involved thirteen precise matches and four errors. For example, two daughters gave excellent descriptions of their mothers' hairstyles on that day. Many remembered such details as how many times they were poked in the heel to draw blood. One baby remembered something tight being taken from around his neck. In turn his mother told how he had been nearly strangled with the umbilical cord.

Dr. Chamberlain cites more than 250 scientific references documenting that the unborn and newborn child can learn and remember everything from specific Dr.

Seuss stories read to him or her prenatally to words like *tinder* or *beagle*. Infants were exposed to these words by researchers because these words would not likely be said by anyone but a researcher studying prenatal memory.

Learning expert Lewis Lipsitt of Brown University has studied newborns and finds that they are "about as competent a learning organism as can be found."

Neonatologist Dr. Thomas Verny adds more fuel to this fire. He tells the story of Boris Brott, a famous conductor who could play certain pieces sight unseen. In conducting a score for the first time, the cello line would jump out at him. So much so at times that he often knew how it went without turning the page. He felt the reason for this uncanny precognition was the fact that his mother was a professional cellist and played many of these pieces over and over again during her pregnancy.

Given the amount of research substantiating infant memory, would it be any kind of surprise to find that people can remember prenatal near-death experiences?

Here are two examples of prenatal NDEs I find extremely difficult to comprehend yet at the same time very convincing.

A DREAM THAT WAS TRUE

A twenty-nine-year-old woman was in the office of one of my colleagues. He happened to mention that I had written a book about near-death experiences.

"What are those?" she asked.

He described them as experiences that happen to people when they die, ones that involve sensations of floating out of the body and entering into a bright light filled with love.

"Oh yeah," she said. "I have those. I never knew what to call them."

That is when he called me.

This woman told me in detail about her recurring dream, one in which she finds herself floating out of her body and entering into a bright light. She said that the dream is vivid and one that constantly reminds her of God. She also said that during the dream she has the sensation of being dead, although she has never really been sick in her life. In her dream she is drawn out of her body through a long dark tunnel and enters into a beautiful and brightly lit place that makes her feel secure. While in this place she has a sense of understanding all of life, yet the precise nature of this understanding escapes her when she awakens.

I was intrigued by this, but even more intrigued by what she told me when she paid me a visit a few months later.

She had never had a good relationship with her father. Despite her description of him as being warm and loving, there was always something about him that brought out anger in her.

One night, when she had the dream again, she asked the light why she could not get along with her father. A voice in the light spoke to her: "Ask your mother about your birth."

A few days later she did just that, telling her mother of the dream and asking what happened during her birth. A torrent of guilt gushed from her mother. "I had no idea that you could remember such a thing. I feel so guilty. I should have told you sooner. When I was eight months pregnant with you, I caught your father in an affair with his secretary. It was so traumatic for me that my placenta separated and you almost died during birth. The doctors really had to work to keep you alive."

This would only be a fanciful story were it not for the exact description of a near-death experience by someone who never knew they were near death and would have no reason to dream of floating out the body, zooming down a tunnel or entering a light, since she didn't even know what a near-death experience was.

Are such dreams common anyway? To answer that question I interviewed two hundred consecutive parents of patients in my pediatric practice, asking them a few simple questions, including this one: *Have you ever had a dream or vision about leaving your physical body, entering into a tunnel, and seeing a bright light?*

Not one of the two hundred patients had ever had such a dream. So certainly we can say that such dreams are not common and that coincidence doesn't seem to be a good explanation for her experience. It seems more likely that her experience was a real one. Given what we now know about the near-death experience and prenatal memory, it seems likely that she was fortunate enough to retain a subconscious memory of her NDE. Within that experience was the understanding of the anger at her father and how to heal it.

This is an area of the near-death experience I am anxious to research. It is my suspicion that adrenaline has a lot to do with the retention of these incredibly early memories. Research has shown that an adrenaline surge which accompanies some kinds of news tends to imprint that information in the neurons, the "gray matter" of memory. This gives us a survival advantage, since it allows us to keep stressful events at the forefront of our thoughts so we can react to them more quickly.

BRIGHT FLASHLIGHT, DARK CAVE

I think these artifacts will someday be examined more closely by researchers. I myself may even try to answer them with studies that will come to conclusive answers—and many more questions still.

I am realistic. I don't expect physicians to become suddenly interested in near-death studies. The excitement I have felt knowing that dying patients are having vivid and real spiritual experiences has provoked very little interest in my medical colleagues. The revolution in how we treat dying patients and patients in intensive-care units has not taken place. Many hospitals are still factories and patients their products.

Medical doctors are not comfortable confronting issues of death and dying. Maybe doctors are just too busy seeing patients and trying to keep up with scientific advances to reflect on the nature of the human soul. I do believe that many physicians are uncomfortable and unprepared to discuss such matters when called upon to do so.

I ran into this discomfort once after speaking to physicians and psychologists at a children's hospital on the West Coast. I had spoken about my experiences with children and then a swarm of us went down to the cafeteria to have lunch. The psychologists spoke freely while the physicians ate in silence.

I began to prod the doctors. What did you think of my talk? I asked.

The head of the intensive-care unit shrugged. "Well, it conflicts with everything I believe to be true. The dying brain cannot have these kinds of images or activity."

Surprisingly, one of the older physicians came to my rescue. "Yes, but how much of what is true do you think we know? Five percent? Ten percent? Certainly what we don't know is far greater than what we do know. Science is like having a very bright flashlight in a gigantic cave."

The head of intensive care put his fork down. He leaned forward and told us a secret.

"I once decided to place a child on a respirator because of a vision that he told me. I was treating an eight-year-old asthmatic. I thought that he was doing okay and was considering sending him home.

"Suddenly he turned to me and said: 'I think I see my grandmother. She's coming for me and I'm going away with her.' The boy's mother said that he was talking nonsense, that the grandmother had died several years ago."

The physician was so shocked by what the boy said that he admitted him to the hospital and began very aggressive treatment. It was lucky that he did. Several hours later he took a turn for the worse and would have died had he not been so close to medical care.

I was astonished to hear this story. Here was the head

of an ICU at a major hospital admitting that a patient's spiritual vision had affected his treatment. Yet he told the story as if discussing a shameful secret. He wanted to make it clear that he didn't believe in things like near-death experiences. And yet he too had discovered an artifact.

Yes, there is much more to look at in the field of near-death studies.

8

The Glow of God

"Only human beings find their way by a light that illuminates more than the patch of ground they stand on."
                    —*Biologists Peter and Jean Medawar*

We covered a lot of ground in the Transformations study. Like all good research, the main question to be answered was a simple one: *Are there transformative effects from the near-death experience that can be documented?* To answer this question we studied adults who had had near-death experiences as children. That way we could look at the long-term effects of NDEs, those changes in physical and psychological makeup that last for years and literally become the core of a person's being.

This study group represented a true cross section of American society. Some were doctors, others were lawyers, real-estate agents, blue collar workers, computer programmers, journalists, artists, housewives, carpenters—virtually every profession possible. Most of the races were represented, including whites, blacks, American Indians, and Hispanics, in comparable percentages as the population as a whole. Also represented were major religions. The only thing the subjects had in common was that at one point in their childhood, they had nearly died.

To prove that some meaningful change had actually taken place, we compared this study group to other adults who had had the same spiritual and religious values and similar physical and psychological traumas. The main difference, of course, was that these other groups had *not* had near-death experiences.

The study revealed a set of profound changes caused by near-death experiences. Even though these people did not know they were different, they were in fact deeply transformed by the most puzzling and spiritual experience most of them have ever had. As one member of the study group declared about the light she saw: "It wasn't God, but it wasn't *not* God."

The light did indeed transform these people, whether they knew it or not. By analyzing the way they live, we could see the very footprints of the near-death experience.

For instance, people who have NDEs exercise more than the "normal" population, eat more fresh fruits and vegetables, use fewer medications like aspirin and other over-the-counter remedies. They also have fewer psychosomatic complaints, miss less time from work, and have fewer years of unemployment than the control groups.

Also, they have fewer hidden symptoms of depression and anxiety than any of the control groups. They spend more time alone in solitary pursuits or in meditation or quiet contemplation. Surprisingly, they spend more quiet time alone than people who describe themselves as New Age humanists.

Those touched by the light at an early age give more of themselves to the community by performing volunteer work. They also give more of their income to charities and are often in helping professions like nursing or special education. Apparently there is some quality in their experience of light that makes them gravitate toward those professions.

THE LAUGHING MORTICIAN

One of my favorite examples of an NDE leading a person to a helping profession is a man I nicknamed "the laughing mortician." When I first met him he was unaware that he had had a near-death experience. He thought I wanted to study people who had nearly died and called to tell me about the time he was electrocuted. When I asked if he had seen a bright light, he quickly denied it. "I did have a really weird dream, but I didn't experience a light."

Here is his story:

"When I was a kid I was playing records in the basement when I reached into the phonograph player and touched some wires. It was as though I was immediately paralyzed. I couldn't move at all.

"The kids who were in the room with me thought I had fainted and went to get some water to throw on me. I knew that couldn't possibly be a good idea and I tried frantically to move or yell or something.

"I felt trapped. But at the same time I realized I was watching myself there on the floor and everything that was going on around me. I was floating out of my body!

"I was fascinated. I watched as paramedics came and put me in an ambulance and took me away to the hospital. Sometimes I would fade out, and everything would be dark. Other times I could hear everything that was going on.

"At the hospital I could see everything they did to me. I saw them put paddles on my chest and say 'stand clear' as they tried to shock life back into me. I seemed to have split vision because while this was going on, I was going down a long tunnel. Along the way I met people who seemed happy to meet me and were talking to me. I didn't know any of them. There were also lots of different doors. I didn't open any of them because I knew they weren't for me. I came to the end of the tunnel which seemed to be in a hazy white mist and I couldn't see anything. It wasn't a light, though. But it was cloudy, misty, and bright.

"At the same time I could see myself below. I could see doctors working on me. I could hear fragments of conversations like, 'we're losing him,' and 'stand clear,' and the like.

"And there was another thing that really puzzled me. There was a woman in the room with me. She was dressed in white and seemed to be a nurse. She didn't speak to the doctors, and held my hand and comforted me. I sensed that everything would be all right. At first I thought that she might have been my mother, but she didn't look like my mother, and anyway, my mother told me later that the doctors told her to wait outside."

He was exactly the type of patient I wanted to study. He was completely naive about the near-death experience, and didn't even know that he had had one. Yet he had all the symptoms of an NDE, including traveling down a tunnel, seeing people, and being bathed in a bright light. Plus, he saw a mysterious woman in white who could certainly be described as a guardian angel or spirit guide.

He embodies the transformative effects of the near-death experience. He gravitated toward a caring profession, but did not know why. "I just chose it. I seem to have a special ability to work with families of those who have died. I really enjoy my work and recognize that I am good at it." Indeed, his bubbly demeanor is why I call him the laughing mortician.

Far from being a touchy-feely weirdo, which is what some cynics call near-death experiencers, he is a man who is actively engaged in the business of living. At the age of forty-one he is half owner of a funeral parlor, a testament to his drive and ambition. He feels that he has a special calling to work with the families of those who have died. His experience left him with the feeling that "there is something more out there," which he feels is a valuable belief to have in helping people overcome grief. "I found that I like working with people who have lost someone," he says. "It seems to be a special gift I have. I've already been through it and it's easy for me to talk to others who are suffering loss."

He figures high on the zest for life index yet extremely low on the death anxiety scale, personality traits that I think were shaped by "that weird dream" he had as a child.

The laughing mortician validates another of my findings: NDEs change the body's electromagnetic field. As

I discussed in an earlier chapter, about half of the people who had valid near-death experiences show signs of an altered electromagnetic nervous system. When I asked him if he ever had trouble wearing a watch, he shrugged and then nodded.

"I can wear a watch," he said. "The problem is that I can't afford to buy a good one, or at least one that keeps running. A friend finally bought me an expensive watch, a Seiko, and even that one doesn't work half the time."

EXPLORED PSYCHIC EVENTS

The Transformations study explored other mysteries of the near-death experience. Perhaps the most intriguing is the fact that psychic and precognitive events happen many times more frequently to NDEers. I find these very pronounced psychic abilities hard to believe. In fact I *would not* believe them if there were not so many of them. When I use a bar graph to compare the number of verifiable psychic experiences, the sheer number of experiences in the study group towers above those of the control group like a skyscraper over a tract home.

Emotionally and professionally, I have trouble believing what I see. There has been nothing in my schooling to prepare me for people who can read minds or who know what is going to happen *before* it happens. In fact there has been much in my schooling that says such a thing cannot happen if for no other reason than it cannot be reproduced in a laboratory.

Yet just when I somehow convince myself to ignore my own scientific data, I run into a near-death experiencer who is so psychic that they are able to tell me intimate details of even my life, things so minute that I have practically forgotten them myself. And then what am I to think, a skeptical inquirer exposed to puzzling events?

I remind myself that these are not people who are trying to trick me into believing they are psychic. These are not people who are trying to polish a Vegas lounge act or get a spot on late night television. Rather, they are normal people who suddenly possess paranormal powers. I realize that such abilities as telepathy and precognition do not in themselves prove the existence of a soul. They could simply be natural human abilities that are poorly understood. After all, we evolved this gigantic brain 200,000 years ago and since it didn't come with an owner's manual we may still be finding new ways to use it.

THE BOTTOM LINE

When I look for the bottom line of the Transformations study and the reality of near-death experiences, I narrow it down to these four points:

The Experience Is Not Like Any Medically Described Hallucinations

NDEs are not like any hallucinations we know of, nor are they akin to drug-induced hallucinations, schizophrenia, transient psychosis, psychotic breaks, anesthetic reactions, or dreams.

The near-death experience is a logical and orderly event that involves floating out of body, entering into darkness and experiencing a wonderful and indescribable light. People who have them know what is happening to them. Unlike people who have hallucinations or episodes of mental illness, NDEers have a feeling of being in control of the situation and do not feel detached from their being.

The real problems begin when people who have had near-death experiences tell others about their marvelous journey, especially members of the medical profession. They are then led to believe that the experience was a hallucination, bad dream, mental illness—anything but the otherworld journey that it really was.

I believe that we doctors are the ones who cannot understand the experience and have an improper perception of someone else's reality. It is the medical profession that is, in a sense, blind to these experiences.

The Near-Death Experience Has Been Independently Verified by Witnesses Whose Testimony Would Be Acceptable in Any Court of Law in the Land

We cannot ignore the powerful stories of those who have shared these experiences with the dying. From the registered nurse who sees the lady in white at the foot of her dying patient's bed, from the mother who simultaneously experiences her dying child's deathbed vision, from the teenage girl who has a vision of her brother's death and shares his NDE ... These people have nothing to gain by inventing these stories. Rather, they expose themselves to ridicule and a variety of unpleasant accusations by bravely stepping forward and talking about these shared experiences.

Does it make sense for medicine to ignore the testimony of these people? Does it make sense to deny the reality of the near-death experience?

The Right Temporal Lobe Is Where the Mind and Body Come Together

The near-death experience probably takes place in the right temporal lobe, a spot just above the right ear and deep within the brain. My research and that of other scientists going back fifty years confirms this spot as the anatomical location of the NDE.

Some people think the experience is lessened by showing where it originates in the brain. I disagree. When we reveal the right temporal lobe as the place in the brain where the NDE occurs, we are talking about the spot where the mind, body, and spirit interact. We are talking about the area that houses the very spark of life itself.

Some researchers believe that the right temporal lobe is an area of the brain that allows us to perceive other realities and perhaps even enter into them. Dr. Michael Schroeter, a philosopher and neuroscientist at the University of Heidelberg in Germany, is one who believes that the right temporal lobe is where the brain, mind, and soul converge in the human body.

When I met Schroeter while lecturing in Germany, he told me of a patient who had a near-death experience and floated out of her body. She saw a ball of light approach her body and listened as her body and the ball of light carried on a conversation. Finally the ball of light said: "You won't join us for another thirty years." She then returned to her body.

This and the many cases like it have led Schroeter,

myself, and others to believe that the temporal lobe is a receiving system, one that allows us to hear voices from a source outside our bodies and perceive the light that comes to us at the point of death.

TRANSFORMED BY THE LIGHT

I have found the experience of light to be the keynote event of the near-death experience, the element that always leads to a transformation. I do believe that the light seen by NDEers comes from a source outside the body.

Why do I believe this? Neuroscientists have documented the existence of these circuit boards of mysticism within our temporal lobes. It is through this neurological machinery that we have the ability to have out-of-body experiences, see white figures, some of whom look like dead relatives, hear heavenly music, have a three-dimensional life review—all the elements of a near-death experience except the transformative experience of light.

It is this loving white light that is the essence of the near-death experience. The other indicators of the near-death experience can be recreated by short-circuiting the right temporal lobe. This was done by Wilder Penfield, the Canadian neurosurgeon, who used electric prods to touch this area of the brain during surgery, thereby producing out-of-body states in patients.

These circuit boards have also been activated by the use of anesthetic drugs such as ketamine, in which patients on the operating table say they are leaving their body. LSD, peyote, and other psychedelic drugs can also trigger some of this circuitry, leading to out-of-body sensations, tunnel experiences, and the like. Yes, I even believe this area of the brain works its magic during periods of intense fear, when a person needs to disassociate from something that is going on or even to slow down time, possibly to avoid an accident.

These building blocks of the spiritual journey can be activated many ways, since they are part of the basic circuitry of our brains.

The experience of light cannot be activated artificially. It is activated only at the point of death or during some very special spiritual visions. This spiritual vision of the loving light results in the personality transformations that we saw in our study group. The most powerful and lasting transformations were seen in people who saw the light.

FEAR DEATH *AND* NEAR DEATH

Let me give you an example of the circuit boards being tripped both ways in the same person, one from fear and the other from near death. This experience was told to me by Dr. van Lummel, a prominent Dutch cardiologist who tells the experience of a patient who nearly died when he rammed into the back of a truck.

During the first stages of the accident, when he realized that collision was imminent, the patient said that time seemed to slow down as he hit the brakes and went into an uncontrolled slide. Then he seemed to pop out of his body. While in this state, he had a life review which consisted of brief pictures—flashes—of his life.

I think this was a "fear death" experience, a dissociative reaction to a life-threatening situation.

What happened next was quite different.

His car struck the truck and the truck bed crashed through the window, causing multiple injuries to his head and chest. Medical reports show that he was in a coma and nearly dead. Yet he had a vivid sensation of leaving his physical body and entering into darkness. He could no longer see the physical world as he could before hitting the truck. He had the feeling of moving up a dark tunnel toward a point of light. Suddenly a being "filled with love and light" appeared to him. Now he had a *second* life review, one guided by the being of light. He felt bathed in love and compassion as he reviewed the moral choices he had made in his lifetime. He suddenly understood that he was an important part of the universe and that his life had a purpose.

It was in the second experience, activated by the process of dying, that he felt transformed by the light as it guided him through his life review. The first life review just seemed to be a succession of pictures. He gained no understanding from viewing them.

DUAL NERVOUS SYSTEM

This story illustrates my belief that we have two nervous systems, each guided by separate portions of our brain. We have the conventional, biochemical nervous system which regulates motor and sensory abilities. It is guided primarily by the left side of our brain and is closely associated with our "internal narrator" which is associated with our left temporal lobe.

The other is a subtle, electromagnetic nervous system which is responsible for healing bone breaks, regeneration of body tissue, and the psychosomatic linkages between the brain and body.

It also accounts for our paranormal abilities, such things as telepathy, precognition, and out-of-body sensations. This is the silent person, the inner conscience, the part of us that communicates with God.

It is within this silent second brain—the circuit boards of mysticism—that we can understand the nature of the near-death experience. When the brain dies and input from the biochemical nervous system ceases, this area of the right temporal lobe turns on, usually for the first time in our lives. It allows us to receive a wonderful and loving light which one patient called "the glow of God."

Those who recover from nearly dying are transformed by this light. They understand that their lives have purpose and meaning, usually involving love of family and mankind in general. They reactivate dormant areas of their brain and discover newly born abilities, both of the paranormal and intuitive variety. They become happy people with hobbies and intellectual pursuits. They spend time alone in meditation. They spend more time in community affairs and helping professions than the "ordinary" population.

Please note what the near-death experience does *not* do. It does not transform the experience into a messianic prophet with a message for mankind. No, these are simple, ordinary people who do not perceive themselves as being any different than anyone else. They do not have any particular religion or philosophy of life, other than to live it to its fullest.

Many times their spiritual transformation changes them so much that they become alienated from their families. They usually view their near-death experience as a private matter, one that they rarely discuss with others. Yet still the transformations occur.

The Near-Death Experience Transforms People Who Have Them

As pointed out above, the experience of light transforms those who have near-death experiences. This transformation is probably the result of a vivid experience of the loving light being imprinted throughout the brain. This memory gives the experiencer a sense of purpose and meaning. Just as the survivor of a near-fatal event *who does not have a near-death experience* will have a bad memory imprinted that results in post traumatic stress syndrome, the NDE creates a post traumatic *bliss* syndrome which results in personality transformation.

That the right temporal lobe is functioning at the point of death is a mystery to some neuroscientists. Yet research suggests that as the brain is dying, portions of the right temporal lobe start to work properly for the first time. The fact that it is processing memory into our long-term memory banks shows that it is working very well.

So then comes the question: What is the energy source that activates this neurological circuitry? As the Russian neuroscientist Vladimer Vladostock points out, the brain in time of coma is desperately trying to save its energy supply and should not be acting to generate complex visions and hallucinations. In an article published in *Critical Care Medicine,* Vladostock concludes that an NDE might be harmful to the dying patient because it contributes to the energy deficit already present. In case after case, patients say that they returned to life after encountering the light and being told that they had to return. The NDE did not rob them of energy, it filled them with it.

RESUSCITATED BY AN NDE

A nurse who had worked at a midwestern hospital for twenty years told me a story that illustrates the resuscitative power of the NDEs.

She said that one of her young patients had a cardiac arrest and nearly died. The resuscitation was plagued with technical problems which ultimately rendered the machinery on the crash cart useless. Yet just as the resuscitation team was giving up, the patient came back to life.

That evening he was angry. He said he was "having fun in heaven," and that he didn't want to return. "But I saw this light and it told me I had to come back to life."

She thought he was delirious. She assured him that it was the doctors that made him come back, not a talking light that he saw in his dreams.

"You're wrong," insisted the boy. "The machine they were trying to use wasn't plugged in. It was God that made me come back." She checked the cords on the crash cart and discovered he was right. Now she believes that he did come back on his own.

Because of the light? I think so. I am convinced, after more than a decade of studying the near-death experience, that this light that comes to us when we die is real. I do not think it is simply a by-product of human brain activity. Rather, I think it is the very source of all we consider to be uniquely human, namely a soul.

The light that comes to us is not simply a reflex spasm of the optic nerve. It is not the stars that we see after banging our head. It is a different kind of light, a light that contains everything in the universe. One woman explained it best when she said that it was not like a light that you see with your eyes. "It was not something I would call 'God,' and yet God was in the light. My grandparents came out of the light and spoke to me, and yet they were part of the light. It wasn't God but it wasn't not God either."

The light that comes at the point of death is real. My studies have proven its existence by showing that it leads to verifiable and reproducible changes in the people who come in contact with it. And the fact that it comes at a time when the brain has little energy of its own points to the possibility that it comes from a source outside the body, independent of human consciousness.

OBVIOUS, NOT EASY

And now at the end, we come back to the basic question: *So what?* "So what are we supposed to do with this information?" ask my colleagues in medicine, many of whom can be as cynical as even the most abrasive radio talk show host.

As a practicing physician, I feel we must leave it to the philosophers and the scientific researchers to discover the true nature of the near-death experience. The next decade will be filled with brilliant consciousness research, much of it examining in detail the circuit boards of mysticism and all the other circuit boards packed into our skulls.

I think our job as physicians is to understand that this experience is real and not caused by drugs. By understanding this experience, we can understand death. As author David Meltzer states so nicely: "Death teaches us to live; it gives us a boundary to map our living within. Death's hammer breaks through the mirror separating us from light."

As a society I feel that our challenge is to use this information in a practical manner when dealing with issues of death and dying. This is especially true when caring for the terminally ill, a ritual that often dehumanizes and degrades the participants.

Dr. William Knaus of George Washington University describes the care of the terminally ill as follows: "In many cases, intrusive and complicated machinery is wheeled in to keep the vital signs going, to give treatment of no benefit and tremendous cost, depriving others of treatment while dignity disappears."

In short, the most important decisions of a patient's life are often made for them—whether or not to be placed on life-support machinery.

I believe that a better understanding of the dying process and a willingness to accept the spiritual visions of the dying would have great impact upon the issue that has become known as the right to die.

These experiences help lessen our fear of death. And by that I mean the fear the doctors feel as well as the dying patients. Psychologist Carl Jung said that our death anxiety leads to an effort to control death, which is exactly what family and physicians are doing when they insist upon life-support systems in the latter days of a terminal illness.

A particularly heartbreaking example of this presented itself to the ethics committee of a hospital.

BOTCHED SUICIDE

Mr. Jones, a fifty-five-year-old man, had suffered for years from a crippling degenerative arthritis. Once an active physical fitness enthusiast who had climbed several mountains, he now watched the world from his wheelchair.

He had made several futile attempts at suicide, but had failed. Those family members who were close to him agreed with his desire to die. However, several family members who lived in another part of the country vehemently opposed his desire to die. This is a pattern I have seen often. Usually the family members least involved in day-to-day care of a dying patient are the ones most eager to prolong life.

Mr. Jones finally convinced his wife to help him die. His days were filled with pain and his nights were ones of the uneasy sleep that narcotics and sleeping pills bring. He and his wife had shared a lifetime of activities like bicycling and hiking. Now they were watching their life savings go into treatment that was doing little to stop his slide into total immobility. Already they had sold their house and moved into a small apartment. With few financial resources remaining, Mr. Jones felt, as the poet Yeats said, like a prisoner trapped in a dying animal. The wife was in complete agreement with his wish to die.

The couple went from doctor to doctor, obtaining a prescription for barbiturates from each one. They plotted along without the help of family, friends, minister, or physician, since they were violating civil and religious law. He made out a living will stating that his life should not be unnaturally prolonged.

Then he took the pills.

When he slipped into a coma, the wife panicked. She called the Emergency Medical Team which resuscitated him while she stood over them asking if such effort was really necessary. In these critical moments she was hopelessly frightened and terribly confused.

At the hospital Mr. Jones was connected to life-support machinery while his case was presented to the ethics committee. His wife wanted him to be removed from life support and allowed to die. Two of the couple's four children wanted him kept on the machinery. One son who lived across the country was sure that his father was simply depressed, and once that depression was treated, would want to live again.

As time passed the man was removed from life support but lived anyway, in a vegetative state. He never returned to consciousness. He survives in an unconscious state to this day.

As one prominent anesthesiologist later told me: "He would have lived better if he had been allowed to die."

Most tragedies like this could be avoided if only we did not fear death so greatly or try to control it so much. The fact that this man had to conspire secretly with his wife, without input from the family physician or minister, is an indictment of our life at any cost philosophy.

As it was the physicians, nurses, wife, and children were all making difficult and agonizing decisions from information based upon their own feelings. An open discussion of euthanasia, death, the fear of dying, and what happens to people when they die could have created a climate in which this family might have arrived at some creative solutions before this man attempted suicide.

CONTROLLING HER DESTINY

A mother wrote to me about a very different case, the death of her seventeen-year-old daughter from necrosis of the liver. The girl's name was Elizabeth and her death seemed particularly tragic since she was a beautiful, bright, and lively girl who graduated from high school at the age of fourteen.

Several months before she died, Elizabeth suffered massive liver failure. At that point, said her mother, she became certain that she was soon going to die. For most people this would be reason to withdraw and become depressed about life. After all, dying young seems to be one of the greatest injustices of all. For Elizabeth, it was reason to rally all the energy that she could.

She told her parents and doctors that she wanted to be in control until the end. She made as many of the decisions about her treatment that she possibly could. She even tried some alternative medicine, including a spiritual healer.

"The possibility of death was talked about quite openly," wrote her mother. "It made some of the nurses and one of the attending physicians furious. But we decided to face each step of the way square on."

Rather than obsess over the cause of her disease, constantly asking the question, "why did this happen to me?" Elizabeth took each day as it came. She struggled to remain clearheaded, despite not being allowed to have pain medication because of the condition of her liver.

"She seemed very clear about her path," wrote her mother. "Toward the end she began to say good-bye to us all. She took each family member aside and told them that she loved them 'bestest of all.' It wasn't until two years later when we all got together for Christmas that we found out what she had done."

Elizabeth weakened for several days and finally slipped into a coma. The day before she died she asked for her journal. She wrote that she had seen the light. She also saw a boundary, "the edge" that the family could not travel beyond. She saw her recently deceased aunt and was able to talk to her about her decision to die soon.

Then she wrote her mother this poem:

I felt the Light was the strong way
And this is the way I'm going to go

But I felt either way and I felt good
There is a cosmic magic which is very simple
And I felt close to both feelings
life and death

I felt part of the spectrum
And just a small part of it.
I feel that I'm allowed to pass through me a
*   statement of*
living and death.
Very important, be sure to write that, too.
I feel rebirth coming and dying
And it's very close
Both, to each other.

In many ways, her last creative act was perhaps her most important one.

I realize that the proper use of pain medication in dying patients is an issue that must be dealt with on an individual basis. Yet most physicians who work with the elderly agree that such patients are often overmedicated as they approach death. Why? Many times it is because heavy sedation makes it easier to control the patient. Often times sedation is done for the sake of the family or the doctor himself. I speak firsthand when I say that the death of a patient is not an easy thing for a doctor to face.

I know it takes more time and is certainly more difficult for the people who must attend to the dying, but I think fewer drugs and more loving care should be offered at the hour of death. I have been involved in many cases where children interpret their own death. Such an exercise is useful in combatting the intense fear and anxiety involved in dying.

AWARENESS, NOT BLACKNESS

How aware of their surroundings are the dying? In the Seattle study, a study I did in 1988 on the psychological events of dying, I found that patients who were *clinically dead* and then were brought back to life did in fact remember their surroundings. To my surprise these patients didn't just go into blackness. Instead they had a substantial amount of control and conscious awareness. Many of these patients report that they are floating out of their physical bodies, very aware of what is going on around them.

This is very important in our treatment of the dying. Where we allow family and friends to visit patients during normal visiting hours, we tend to exclude family members from the bedside at the actual time of death. We need to reverse these policies, making the bedside more crowded with people and less crowded with machines.

For example, a close friend of mine recently witnessed his grandfather die in a hospital of a heart attack. He was greatly disturbed at the thought that his grandfather died in great pain. Yet based upon scientific research, I was able to convince him that his grandfather probably perceived his own death as being peaceful, even spiritual.

My friend then told me that *his* father was haunted by the fact that he could not say good-bye to his father. He had visited the hospital many times, but when the heart attack struck, the doctors jammed the room and he was told to leave. When he finally gathered his courage and went into the room anyway, his father had died.

Once again I pointed to the scientific research. I told him that his father probably did see him saying good-bye. Even though he could not respond, he was probably aware that his son was there and wanted to offer his final farewell.

I did not tell him that his father was in heaven. I only told him what I could back up as a scientist: that his father may well have seen him in his dying moments.

This is an example of what it means to mix spirituality and science. By doing this we return a greater sense of control to patients and their families. We also help validate the spiritual feelings and intuitions that so many people still ignore because they are afraid they will be ridiculed by science-minded physicians. I feel that there is enough scientific data to validate these experiences as real. I think physicians should share this information with patients and their families, make them feel comfortable about predeath visions, near-death experiences, and other spiritual phenomena, tell them about this data and let them make up their own minds.

A SHINING MOMENT

A chaplain recently described how she used her knowledge of near-death experiences to help empower a patient and her family. The patient was an old woman dying of cancer. Her sisters were at her bedside. The woman rallied on the last day and spoke to her sisters. "Tom is here," she said pointing at the foot of the bed. "Oh at last, Tom is here."

"Who is Tom?" asked the chaplain.

The sisters were embarrassed. They tried to quiet the dying woman who was quite excited and still pointing.

"She doesn't know what she's saying," said one of the sisters. "Tom is her husband. He has been dead for twenty years."

The chaplain surprised them with her response. "Where do you think Tom would be if not here?" she asked.

The attitude of the women changed. Rather than reject the deathbed vision of their sister, they participated in it. "Show us where Tom is," said one of the women. They both gathered around her in the bed and looked at Tom until their beloved sister died.

This moment of acceptance made a tremendous difference for these two women. Instead of their final memories being of their sister raving from hallucinations and talking out of her head as she died, they had a powerful moment in which they were able to help their sister with the process of dying. They shared in her vision. And as a result, the grieving process was made an easier one for them.

This chaplain was comfortable with death and confident in her own spirituality. She did not attempt to interpret the experience for the sisters or let her own beliefs intrude into this very delicate moment. All she did was suggest that Tom was in fact at the bedside and that only the dying person could see him. The sisters themselves knew it was Tom. They were simply unable to act on their intuition until the chaplain, the official in the room, gave them permission.

HEARTFELT EXPERIENCE

Understanding and accepting spiritual experiences can prevent pathological grieving, even when it is someone else's experience.

I said this at a conference in Sweden and was approached later by a pediatric cardiologist who disagreed. "People can't share these experiences, even with their children," she said. "How can people benefit from something that they themselves cannot perceive?"

I was shocked at what she said and did the best I could to respond. I explained to her that when a child dies, the natural order of the universe is turned upside down for the parents. They become angry at the hand fate has dealt them and it is very difficult to channel their rage into healthy pathways. She never did understand what I was getting at.

For instance, I had a patient who was born with a severe brain disorder that causes the brain to die slowly. The parents had a very difficult time understanding why their child was dying. They intended to blame themselves with irrational guilt since the true cause of this horrible disorder is not known. The mother had used cocaine early in the pregnancy and was convinced that her drug use was the cause. The father, on the other hand, thought the brain disorder was caused by bad genes that he had passed on.

In the midst of all this, the mother began to talk about a vision she had had before the baby was born. She was awakened in the middle of the night by a lady in white who said, "Your baby was not meant to be and must come back with me now."

I tried to get them both to accept that as the explanation for their child's fatal illness. What better explanation could there be, I asked, than that this baby was not meant to be?

Rather than accept this spiritual vision, the parents became more bitter and angry. When I think of them I am reminded of the Zen parable about the man who searched for fire with a lighted candle. Had he known the nature of fire, his search would surely have been shorter.

Had this couple been willing to accept the vision, their anger and unhappiness would have been shorter, too.

TRUSTING THE VISION

Listen to what one mother wrote to me about the last few months of her son who was dying of cancer at home. He had spiritual visions in which he anticipated his own death. By the time this happened, he had lost his hair from chemotherapy and was nothing but skin and bones. He wanted to stop treatment because of the visions. His mother agreed and with the permission of his doctors he withdrew from treatment and went home.

I had asked her to describe what it was like to have her son die at home. Here was her reply:

"You asked what it was like to be at the bedside of a dying child. That made me laugh because Sean died on the living room floor. The last few weeks he was very restless and wanted to be on the sofa or the big chair or on his sleeping bag on the floor. If he had been in the hospital we couldn't have done that. I really don't know exactly what you are asking.

"If you mean, how did it feel emotionally, it was the most terrifying and at the same time the most moving thing I've ever experienced. It was awful to see my child grow sicker and weaker day by day and to be able to do absolutely nothing to stop it from happening. At the same time it was wonderful to be able to care for him, hold him when he wanted it, fix his favorite foods, even if he didn't eat it, watch him wait anxiously for 3 P.M. when his sisters came home, all things that couldn't have happened if he was in the hospital.

"It required every ounce of strength I had to get through it. Sometimes I felt like I was going to explode into a million pieces and often I wished that I could die too, even though I knew that wasn't fair to my husband and my daughters. I don't know what my husband felt during this time. I have never asked him.

"I really believe that if the parents are not ready or willing to let the child go, then the dying can drag on and on. . . . Most parents that I've talked to were not like us though. They wanted to try everything up to the bitter end even if there was almost no chance. These parents seem to have a harder time grieving.

"One lady that I've been writing to has an eight-year-old daughter who died of leukemia. The doctors told her it was fatal, but she said they wanted to try it all. That girl went through hell. She was in the hospital for most of her last six months while doctors tried radiation, chemotherapy, and all kinds of things. Just before the girl died, she said: 'I failed. I'm sorry.'

"After Sean died, no one wanted to talk about it. Most

Americans are terrified about death. It leaves us bereaved parents in a very bad state."

This mother believed in her child's visions and was transformed by it as much as if she herself had experienced it.

CLINICAL APPLICATIONS

As a clinician, my main interest in near-death experiences is from a practical viewpoint, mainly, how can this information be used to help patients? I think my research, which focuses first on the patient, has allowed me to see things that other investigators have missed.

I had expected the typical near-death experiencer to be a touchy-feely, "blissed-out" New Ager. Instead I found that people who have near-death experiences are usually ordinary people who survive an extraordinary experience.

Now, after more than a decade of research, I have seen the powerful effects of the experience in the many ways in which it changes people. Does this research have a clinical application, something families, doctors, and caregivers can use to help those coping with death and dying?

I have developed a series of guidelines to help people coping with these experiences to understand better what is going on and what they can do to promote sympathy and support. I do not believe it is necessary for health-care professionals to take sides in the debate concerning the objective reality of these spiritual experiences, but I do think it is necessary to realize that they are a natural and normal part of the dying process and have profound implications for those of us who work with death and dying.

To help people understand these experiences, I have developed these implications for all who might be concerned with this experience.

Implications for the Dying Patient

1. The near-death experience (NDE) validates the patient's own psychical experiences and can restore control and dignity to the process of dying.
2. The knowledge that the process of dying is not painful or scary, but spiritual and wondrous, can be comforting.
3. Comatose patients often are able to hear and see everything that is going on around them, and can emotionally process conversations. Often they subjectively perceive themselves to be floating on the ceiling and perceive themselves to have a bird's-eye view of their own deathbed or resuscitation.
4. If the dying patient has had spiritual visions, these can be used to interpret the process of dying for them. There is no need to dismiss such visions or intuitions as drug-induced experiences or hallucinations.
5. For patients who have not had death-related visions, guided imagery or fantasy can often serve the same purpose.
6. Knowledge of near-death experiences can reverse the isolation and neglect of the dying. People will want to visit to hear about predeath visions or to work

with guided imagery with the dying. The old-fashioned deathbed scene crowded with relatives and friends may be resurrected.

Implications for Surviving Family and Friends

1. Research on near-death experiences validates a variety of death-related visions. The knowledge that near-death experiences are "real" events can bring new meaning to a peaceful smile before death, a faraway look in the eyes, or simple and brief statements such as "the light, the light" that might otherwise be dismissed.
2. Frequently friends and family members have postdeath visions and intuitions that can be properly interpreted in light of this new scientific information. For example, Dr. Therese Rando states that 75 percent of grieving parents have postdeath hallucinations of their dying child. Simply restating that most parents will see their child again after death without using a medical term such as *hallucination* can bring enormous comfort and give the parent permission to interpret the event in their own way.
3. Death-related visions can serve to restore a sense of control and order to the universe, which is particularly important in dealing with untimely deaths or the death of a child.
4. Death-related visions can promote healthy grieving and decrease the incidence of pathological grief, by decreasing guilt and the sense of personal responsibility that can interfere with normal grieving.
5. Death-related visions generate a sense of meaning

for death, even if that meaning is elusive. For example, a predeath vision of a child's accidental death can allow parents to feel there is some meaning to the death. This can convert a senseless tragedy to a senseful one, which again is helpful in preventing pathological grief.

6. Family and friends can find comfort in knowledge that those last moments of life are serene and peaceful in spite of the reality of the dehumanization and seeming torture of critical-care medicine.

7. Knowledge that it is now scientifically possible to entertain the survival hypothesis can give hope for eventually becoming reunited with the dying. This can be extraordinarily comforting for many.

8. Death-related visions can give faith and confidence to survivors to trust their own spiritual intuitions and reaffirm their religious faith.

Implications for Health Professionals

1. Death-related visions can play a similar role for us in alleviating our own guilt, lack of control, and spiritual/social isolation when dealing with death and dying.

2. Death-related visions can relieve us of a sense of responsibility and the need to always be in control, always have the right answer, the right dose of medicine, etc., when confronted with the deaths of our patients.

3. Ultimately, we may see a decreased need for irrational adherence to rules and policies that reflect our

own need to impose control and order on the process of dying instead of focusing on patient care needs.

4. Death related visions or the use of guided imagery with the dying can result in increased bedside activities, conversations about death and dying, touching, holding, and simply sitting; all which can reverse the social isolation of the dying.

5. What should I say to a patient or one of the family members about a death-related vision?

- Analyze your own spiritual beliefs and feelings about death. Dismissing a patient's visions of the afterlife as ravings and hallucinations can often reflect our own religious beliefs and values.
- When in doubt, do and say nothing.
- Recognize that most death-related events are not dramatic visions of an afterlife, but might be simple feelings and intuitions. Patients are often troubled if they do not have a dramatic vision of another life.
- Encourage discussion among family and friends. Often death-related visions and their significance only become evident when several family members report having the same experience at the same time. A professional willing to validate the experience as normal and natural can often give the family permission to trust their instincts and beliefs.
- Family members often perceive comatose patients as stuck in the tunnel. Others want to know why their child or spouse did not choose to return to them. These issues must be addressed in an individual manner, but are common perceptions.

- Resist the urge to have all the answers or interpret the experiences. The whole point is to surrender control to the dying and their family.

6. Recognize that near-death experiences may make death more attractive to those considering suicide. However, those who have attempted suicide and have had near-death experiences return to life with the firm conviction that suicide is not a solution.

KNOWLEDGE CAN TRANSFORM

The knowledge that these visionary experiences at the point of death are real and transformative validates us as spiritual beings. These experiences teach us many things, but most important they show us that there is a fountain of life from which all of us spring. So many of society's problems—drug addiction, depression, the chaos and despair of inner cities, and the environmental disasters we are inflicting upon ourselves—speak to a lack of understanding that all of life is interconnected and with purpose.

Human beings have the ability to be inspired by a light which has the power to transform them. We do not have to die to learn from this experience. We only have to be open to its message.

I have never heard that message better described than by Jaimal Lovitt, a high school student who wrote this describing the light:

"I once saw the Light, it was not like anything you could imagine, for it was like a sound that existed only in the silence of pitch black. It is the sound of life searching for a place to lay and rest, almost as if it was everybody's existing energy taken and mixed together to form a white ball of Light that rings the sound of life as loud as it can, but so faint that the unaware don't hear it and the aware only think they do.

"The Light is a pattern that some call life. The ups and downs, the happy the sad, the good the bad, the only thing that is real and not quite in our reach, the people who talk and then lose their speech. The quiet of the afternoon, the thought that the end is soon. The calling of the world to shout out and scream, 'I'm alive, can't you see, so give me the power to hear the great sound for I've heard it once it won't let me down.'

"I shall see the Light as white as it may be, but when I die it shall always be with me. For when it's all over, old and turned gray, my Light will be there forever to stay because it is neverending, eternal and sharp, and it will always be with me even in the everlasting dark."

Appendix

The Transformations Study Data

A total of 350 adults were interviewed for the Transformations study. We interviewed 100 adults who had near-death experiences as children and 50 patients in each of the control groups.

We found our study subjects through word-of-mouth, newspaper advertisements, notices on bulletin boards, and radio and television programs. The groups were sex matched and age matched, with roughly equal numbers of adults in the following groups: 20–30 year-olds, 31–40, 41–50, 51–60, 61–70, and 70 and over.

The study groups were as follows:

- Adults who as children were both seriously ill and had near-death experiences (NDEs).
- Adults who were seriously ill as children, but had no NDEs.
- Adults who identify themselves as having an interest in NDEs or identify themselves as having New Age values, yet have never been seriously ill or had a mystical or visionary experience.

239

- Adults who have had simple out-of-body experiences as adults or as children.
- Normal adults, mostly the parents of my patients in a suburban, predominantly white middle-class practice.
- Adults who had mystical or visionary experiences as children but not in the context of illness.

The entire battery of tests given to the subjects took an average of three hours to complete. There were both open-ended questions and essay questions, as well as formal psychological testing instruments.

All the patients gave their informed consent and agreed to allow their case histories to be presented in this book as well as in the scientific papers that will spring from the research. Absolute confidentiality was promised to them; therefore many details of the case histories have been altered, including descriptions of disease, age, and sex.

The complete test consisted of the following:

- The Ellsworth Profile of Adaptation to Life Survey.
- A lifestyle profile: questions regarding exercise habits, nutritional history, educational and occupational history, family history, and marital history.
- A complete medical and psychiatric history.
- A religious and spiritual profile: a combination of essay questions and formal rating scales.
- The Greyson Value Survey: essay questions and formal rating scales dealing with personal feelings and views on a variety of topics, including marriage, money, sex, and business.
- The Greyson Near-Death Experience Validity Scale: a scale that is designed to determine if a person truly has had an NDE.

- The Templer Death Anxiety Scale: a test that shows the level of a person's fear of death.
- A family bonding and rating scale.
- The Reker-Peacock Life Attitude Profile.
- The Greyson Negative Near-Death Experience Inventory.
- The Neppe Subjective Paranormal Events Questionnaire.
- The Neppe Temporal Lobe Sensitivity Inventory (INSET).

RESULTS

Greyson Near-Death Experience Validity Scale Test Scores

Child NDE (CNDE)	13.7
Child Illness (CI)	3.25
Psychic/New Age (P/NA)	6.1
Out of Body (OBE)	12.4
Normal Control (NC)	2.9
Vision (or Dream of Light) (V)	18.1

This test is meant to show the validity of a near-death experience. But the significance of these findings is that the Greyson near-death validity scale cannot distinguish between near-death experiences and visionary or spiritual experiences of any source.

Templer Death Anxiety Scale Test Scores

CNDE	5.4
CI	6.7

P/NA   6.8
OBE   6.25
NC   6.8
V   3.7

The significance of these results is that visions of light or near-death experiences result in lowered death anxiety. The simple out-of-body state did not lead to lowered death anxiety, a finding consistent with Twemlow's research. Simply having an interest in near-death experiences or New Age thinking does not seem to lower death anxiety.

Greyson Value Survey Test Scores

	CNDE	CI	P/NA	OBE	NC	V
Personal/material	5.5	7.2	6.2	7.2	6.6	4.2
Social	12.3	12.1	11.7	13.0	12.5	12.0
Political	12.2	12.1	11.2	13.0	11.75	12.0
Spiritual/altruistic	10.2	9.8	12.3	11.3	10.3	9.8

The significance of these results is that having an NDE, OBE, or visionary experience does not seem to alter one's professed values. These surveys are simply laundry lists of what the subject believes is important. I think that many of us agree on paper about what the proper values in life are. It is actually living up to those values that is important. There is a slight tendency for those having had NDEs or other visionary experiences to value the personal and material less than those who have not had these experiences.

Ellsworth Profile of Adaptation to Life Test Scores

	CNDE	CI	P/NA	OBE	NC	V
Social Activity	9.5	6.2	7.7	8.1	7.6	7.8
Private Activity	10.7	8.0	8.2	9.2	7.1	8.2
Nutrition and Exercise	10.5	5.5	9.0	8.5	6.5	9.0
Personal Growth	8.0	5.0	7.0	6.3	4.8	7.0
Spiritual Awareness	19.9	15.2	17.0	18.0	16.2	17.0

Overall, those who had childhood NDEs generally score better in all categories, including psychosomatic complaints, drug use, and income management. However, it is in the life-style indexes that we truly see the transformations caused by the NDE. In every category, from social activity to nutrition and exercise to spiritual awareness, those who had childhood NDEs radiate well-being. The authors of the PAL test comment that the life-style and spiritual beliefs of well-adjusted people tend to be different from those of poorly adjusted people.

In this test we see for the first time the differences between having a vision or a dream of light and actually having an NDE. The former, a neurophysiological dry run, can lower death anxiety, and may suggest to the experiencer that something else exists after death, but only as a vague perception. The subject who survives an NDE is irrevocably altered for life.

Neppe Subjective Paranormal Events Questionnaire Test Scores

	CNDE	CI	P/NA	OBE	NC	V
Validated	4.1	1.4	1.7	1.6	0.5	3.0
Unvalidated	4.8	3.7	5.8	2.8	2.8	4.4

This test shows that by activating the portion of the brain that is thought to be responsible for psychic activity, a four-fold increase in verifiable psychic experiences is recorded. Yet those people who had the visions of light and out-of-body experiences also have the same psychical area activated.

BIBLIOGRAPHY

Abrams, Jeremiah. *Reclaiming the Inner Child*. Jeremy P. Tarcher Inc., Los Angeles, 1990.

Ader, Robert. *Psychoneuroimmunology*. Academic Press, San Diego, 1991.

Agerskov, Michael. *Toward the Light*. Toward the Light Pub., Denmark, 1979.

Andereasen, Nancy C., M.D. *The Broken Brain*. Harper & Row, New York, 1984.

Anderson, George. *We Don't Die*. Berkley Books, New York, 1988.

Aries, Philippe. *Centuries of Childhood*. Vintage, New York, 1962.

Aries, Philippe. *Western Attitudes Towards Death*. The Johns Hopkins University Press, Baltimore, 1974.

Aries, Philippe. *The Hour of Our Death*. Alfred A. Knopf, New York, 1981.

Armstrong, Thomas. *The Radiant Child*. Theosophical Pub. House, England, 1985.

Atkinson, Rita L., Atkinson, Richard C., Smith, Edward E., and Bem, Daryl J. *Introduction to Psychology*. 10th ed. Harcourt Brace Jovanovich, San Diego, 1990.

Atwater, P.M.H. *Coming Back to Life*. Ballantine Books, New York, 1988.

Baer, D. M. "The temporal lobes: an approach to the study of organic behavior changes," in *Handbook of Behavioral Neurobiology*, vol. 2, Gazzaniga, M.S., ed. *New York Plenum*, 1979.

banLeent, Thea. *De aarde is 'Slechts' een leerschool*.

Uitgeberij Akasha Eeserveen, Grafimix, Drouwen, 1991.

Bauman, Edward. *The Holistic Health Handbook.* Berkeley Press, Calif., 1978.

Becker, Ernest. *The Denial of Death.* Free Press, New York, 1973.

Becker, Robert O., M.D., and Selden, Gary. *The Body Electric.* William Morrow & Co., New York, 1985.

Bhaktivedanta, Swami Prabhupada. *Bhagavad-gita as It Is.* Collier Books, New York, 1972.

Birnbaum, Raoul. *The Healing Buddha.* Shambhala, Boulder, Colo., 1979.

Bluebond-Langer, Myra. *The Private Worlds of Dying Children.* Princeton University Press, N.J., 1978.

Bragdon, Emma. *The Call of Spiritual Emergency.* Harper & Row, New York, 1990.

Bramblett, John. *When Good-bye is Forever: Learning to Live Again after the Loss of a Child.* Ballantine Books, New York, 1991.

Brim, Orville G., Jr., et al. *The Dying Patient.* Russell Sage Foundation, New York, 1970.

Buber, Martin. *Ecstatic Confessions.* Harper & Row, New York, 1985.

Bucke, Richard Maurice, M.D. *Cosmic Consciousness.* Citadel Press, New York, 1989.

Buckingham, Robert W. *Care of the Dying Child.* Continuum, New York, 1989.

Buckley, Heather. *When Your Dead, Your Livin.* 405 Knoll Lane, Brooking, OR 97415, San Jose, CA, 1986.

Burnham, Sophy. *A Book of Angels.* Ballantine Books, New York, 1990.

Callahan, Roger. *Why Do I Eat When I Am Hungry?* Doubleday, New York, 1991.

Calvin, William H. *The Cerebral Symphony.* Bantam Books, New York, 1989.

Campbell, Joseph. *The Mysteries.* Princeton Univ. Press, N.J., 1955.

Campbell, Joseph. *Myths to Live By.* Bantam Books, New York, 1972.

Campbell, Joseph. *The Power of Myth.* Doubleday, New York, 1988.

Campbell, Joseph. *Transformations of Myth Through Time.* Harper & Row, New York, 1990.

Carlson, Eric T., et al. *Hallucinations.* Arno Press, New York, 1976.

Chamberlain, David. *Babies Remember Birth.* Jeremy P. Tarcher Inc., Los Angeles, 1988.

Changeux, Jean-Pierre. *Neuronal Man.* Oxford Univ. Press, New York, 1985.

Chopra, Deepac, M.D. *Quantum Healing.* Bantam Books, New York, 1990.

Coles, Robert. *The Spiritual Life of Children.* Houghton Mifflin Co., Boston, 1990.

Cornwell, John. *The Hiding Places of God.* Warner Books, New York, 1991.

Cranston, Sylvia, and Williams, Carey. *Reincarnation: A New Horizon in Science, Religion and Society.* Julian Press, New York, 1984.

d'Abro, A. *The Evolution of Scientific Thought.* Dover Publications, New York, 1950.

Dass, Ram. *The Only Dance There Is.* Anchor Books, New York, 1974.

David-Neel, Alexandra. *Magic and Mystery in Tibet.* Dover Publications, New York, 1971.

Deloria, Vine, Jr. *Black Elk Speaks.* University of Nebraska Press, Lincoln, 1961.

Dennett, Daniel C. *The Minds I.* Bantam Books, New York, 1981.

Dept. of Health, Education, and Welfare. *Medicine in Chinese Cultures.* Geographic Health Studies, Seattle, 1974.

Doore, Gary. *What Survives?* Jeremy P. Tarcher Inc., Los Angeles, 1990.

Dossey, L. *Meaning and Medicine: A Doctor's Tales of Breakthrough and Healing.* Bantam Books, New York, 1991.

Dossey, L. *Space, Time and Medicine.* Shambhala, Boston, 1982.

Ducasse, C. J. *Nature Mind and Death.* Open Court Pub. Co., Peru, Ill., 1951.

Eastman, Peggy, and Barr, John L., M.D. *Your Child Is Smarter Than You Think.* William Morrow & Co., New York, 1985.

Eby, Richard E. *Caught Up into Paradise.* Fleming H. Revell Co., Tarrytown, N.J., 1978.

Eby, Richard E. *Tell Them I Am Coming.* Fleming H. Revell Co., Tarrytown, N.J., 1980.

Eddy, Mary Baker. *Science and Health with Key to the Scriptures.* The First Church of Christ, Boston, Mass., 1906.

Ekstrom, Margarita. *Death's Midwives.* Ontario Review Press, Princeton, 1985.

Eliade, Mircea. *Shamanism: Archaic Techniques of Ecstasy.* Princeton Univ. Press, N.J., 1964.

Elmer, Lon. *Why Here Why Now.* Bantam Books, New York, 1987.

Evans-Wentz, W. Y., ed. *The Tibetan Book of the Dead.* Oxford Univ. Press, New York, 1960.

Feifel, Herman. *New Meanings of Death.* McGraw-Hill Book Co., New York, 1977.

Ferris, T. *The Mind's Sky: Human Intelligence in a Cosmic Context.* Bantam, New York, 1992.

Feynman, Richard. *The Character of Physical Law.* MIT Press, Cambridge, Mass., 1965.

Forti, Kathleen. *The Door to the Secret City.* Stillpoint Pub., Walpole, N.H., 1984.

Franklin, Jon. *Molecules of the Mind.* Laurel, New York, 1987.

Furst, Peter T. *Hallucinogens and Culture.* Chandler & Sharp Pubs., Novato, Calif., 1976.

Gardner, Howard. *The Mind's New Science.* Basic Books, New York, 1985.

Glasser, William, M.D. *Stations of the Mind.* Harper & Row, New York, 1981.

Gorer, M. *Death, Grief and Mourning.* Anchor Books, New York, 1967.

Gould, Stephen Jay. *The Flamingo's Smile: Reflections in Natural History.* W. W. Norton, New York, 1985.

Graham, Billy. *Facing Death and the Life After.* Word Books, 1987.

Grey, Margot. *Return from Death.* Arkana, New York, 1985.

Grof, Stanislav, M.D., and Halifax, Joan. *The Human Encounter With Death.* Dutton, New York, 1977.

Grof, Stanislav, and Grof, Christina. *Beyond Death.* Thames and Hudson, England, 1980.

Grof, Stanislav. *East and West: Ancient Wisdom and Modern Science.* Broadside Editions, San Francisco, 1983.

Grosso, Michael. *The Final Choice.* Stillpoint Pub., Walpole, N.H., 1985.

Hall, Edward T. *The Hidden Dimension.* Anchor Books, New York, 1966.

Harner, Michael. *The Way of the Shaman.* Harper, San Francisco, 1990.

Harris, Barbara, and Bascom, Lionel C. *Full Circle.* Pocket Books, New York, 1990.

Hart, M., and Stevens, J. *Drumming at the Edge of Magic.* Harper San Francisco, 1990.

Hawking, Stephen W. *A Brief History of Time.* Bantam Books, New York, 1988.

Hobson, J. Allan. *The Dreaming Brain.* Basic Books, New York, 1988.

Hofmann, Albert. *LSD My Problem Child.* Jeremy P. Tarcher Inc., Los Angeles, 1983.

Hofstadter, Douglas R. *Gödel, Escher, Bach: An Eternal Golden Braid.* Vintage, New York, 1979.

Holbrook, Bruce. *The Stone Monkey.* William Morrow & Co., New York, 1981.

Hooper, Judith, and Teresi, Dick. *The Three Pound Universe.* Laurel, New York, 1986.

James, William. *The Varieties of Religious Experience.* The Modern Library, New York, 1902.

Jaynes, Julien. *The Origin of Consciousness and the Breakdown of the Bicameral Mind.* Houghton Mifflin Co., Boston, 1976.

John Dafree. *Easy Death.* The Dawn Horse Press, Clearlake, Calif., 1983.

Jung, C. G. *Modern Man in Search of a Soul.* Harcourt Brace Jovanovich, New York, 1933.

Jung, C. G. *Psychology and the Occult.* Princeton University Press, N.J. 1977.

Kalish, R. A. *Death, Grief, and Caring Relationships.* Brooks/Cole, Pacific Grove, Calif., 1985.

Kappraff, Jay. *Connections.* McGraw-Hill Publishing Co., New York, 1991.

Kastenbaum, Robert. *Between Life and Death.* Springer Pub. Co., New York, 1979.

Kastenbaum, Robert. *Is There Life After Death?* Prentice Hall, Englewood Cliffs, N.J., 1984.

Kleinman, Arthur. *Patients and the Healers and the Context of Culture.* Univ. of California Press, Berkeley, 1980.

Klink, Joanne. *Vroeger toenik Groot was.* Ten Have/ Baarne, Schoten, 1990.

Koocher, Gerald P., and O'Malley, John E., M.D. *The Damocles Syndrome.* McGraw-Hill Publishing Co., New York, 1981.

Kramer, Kenneth. *The Sacred Art of Dying.* Paulist Press, New York, 1988.

Kubler-Ross, Elizabeth, and Warshaw, M. *To Live Until We Say Good-bye.* Prentice Hall, Englewood Cliffs, N.J., 1978.

Kubler-Ross, Elizabeth. *Death: The Final Stage of Growth.* Prentice Hall, Englewood Cliffs, N.J., 1985.

Kubler-Ross, Elizabeth. *On Children and Death.* Macmillan Pub. Co., New York, 1983.

Kunz, Dora. *Spiritual Aspects of the Healing Arts.* Theosophical Publishing House, England, 1985.

Kutscher, Austin H. *Death and Bereavement.* Charles C. Thomas Pub., Springfield, Ill. 1969.

Lauf, Detlef Ingo. *Secret Doctrines of the Tibetan Books of the Dead.* Shambhala, London, 1977.

Lee, Jung Young. *Death and Beyond in the Eastern Perspective.* Gordon & Breach, New York, 1974.

Leming, Michael R., and Dickinson, George E. *Understanding Dying, Death, and Bereavement.* Holt, Rinehart & Winston, Fort Worth, Tex., 1990.

Lesley, Craig. *Talking Leaves.* Laurel, New York, 1991.

Levine, Stephen. *Meetings at the Edge.* Anchor Books, New York, 1984.

Levine, Stephen. *Who Dies?* Anchor Books, New York, 1982.

Lundahal, Craig R. *A Collection of Near-Death Research Readings.* Nelson-Hall, Chicago, Ill., 1982.

Lynch, James J. *The Broken Heart: The Medical Consequences of Loneliness.* Basic Books, New York, 1977.

MacDonald, Hope. *When Angels Appear.* Daybreak Books, Grand Rapids, Mich., 1982.

Macdonald-Cornford, Francis (trans). *The Republic of Plato.* Oxford Univ. Press, New York, 1970.

McMahan, Forrest R. *Near Death.* The Synergetics Press, Parkersburg, W.Va., 1985.

Maguire, Jack. *The Guide to Your Gray Matter: Care and Feeding of the Brain.* Doubleday Pub., New York, 1990.

Majno, Guido. *The Healing Hand.* Harvard University Press, Cambridge, Mass., 1975.

Marion, Robert, M.D. *The Boy Who Felt No Pain.* Addison-Wesley Publishing Co., New York, 1990.

Martin, J. and Romanowski, P. *We Are Not Forgotten.* Appendix 1: The Electroencephalogram Test. G. P. Putnam's Sons, New York, 1991.

Mascaro, Juan. *The Bhagavad Gita.* Penguin Books, New York, 1962.

Maslow, A. H. *The Farther Reaches of Human Nature.* Viking, New York, 1971.

Meduna, L. J., M.D. *Carbon Dioxide Therapy.* Charles C. Thomas Pub., Springfield, Ill., 1950.

Meltzer, David. *Death: An Anthology of Ancient Text, Songs, Prayers, and Stories.* North Point Press, San Francisco, 1984.

Mendell, Arnold. *Coma Key to Awakening.* Shambhala, Boston, 1989.

Michael, Max, III, M.D., et al. *Biomedical Bestiary: An Epidemiologic Guide to Flaws and Fallacies in the Medical Literature.* Little, Brown & Co., Boston, 1984.

Mishlove, Jeffrey. *The Roots of Consciousness.* Random House, New York, 1975.

Moody, Raymond A., Jr., M.D. *Coming Back.* Bantam, New York, 1990.

Moody, Raymond A., Jr. *Elvis After Life: Unusual Psychic Experiences Surrounding the Death of a Superstar.* Peachtree Press, Atlanta, 1987.

Moody, Raymond A., Jr., M.D. *The Light Beyond.* Bantam Books, New York, 1988.

Moody, Raymond A., Jr., M.D. *Life After Life.* Bantam Books, New York, 1975.

Moody, Raymond A., Jr., M.D. *Reflections on Life After Life*. Bantam Books, New York, 1977.

Morse, Melvin. *Closer to the Light*. Ivy Books, New York, 1990.

Noyes, R. "Near-Death Experiences: Their Interpretation and Significance," in Kastenbaum, R., ed. *Between Life and Death*. New York, Springer Publishing Company, 1979.

Olsen-Kelly-Mary, eds. *The Fireside Treasury of Light*. Simon & Schuster, New York, 1990.

Ornstein, Robert E. *The Psychology of Consciousness*. Penguin Books, England, 1972.

Ornstein, Robert, and Sobel, David, M.D. *The Healing Brain*. Touchstone Books, New York, 1987.

Oyler, Chris, and Becklund, Polson. *Go Toward the Light*. Penguin Books, New York, 1988.

Padgett, James E. *Angelic Revelations of Divine Truth*. Foundation Church of the Divine Truth, Washington, D.C., 1988.

Padus, Emrika. *Your Emotions and Your Health*. Rodale Press, Emmaus, Pa., 1986.

Peat, F. David. *Synchronicity: the Bridge Between Matter and Mind*. Bantam Books, New York 1987.

Plum, F., and Posner, J.B. *Diagnosis of Stupor and Coma (edition 2)* F. A. Davis Co., Philadelphia, 1972.

Plum, Fred, and Posner, Jerome B. *Diagnosis of Stupor and Coma*. F. A. Davis Co., Philadelphia, 1972.

Popescu, Petru. *Amazon Beaming*. Viking, New York, 1991.

Popp, Fritz Albert. *Electromagnetic Bioinformation*. Urban & Schwarzenberg, Baltimore, 1989.

Preston, Betty. *Fear Not*. Ibbybooks, Seattle, 1991.

Probonsha, Jack W., M.D. *Is Death for Real?* Pacific Press Pub. Ass., Boise, Ind., 1981.

Rando, Therese A. *Parental Loss of a Child*. Research Press, Champaign, Ill., 1986.

Ratner, Ellen. *The Other Side of the Family*. Health Communications Inc., Deerfield Beach, Fla., 1990.

Rawlings, M. *Beyond Death's Door*. Nelson, Nashville, 1978.

Reiff, Robert, and Scheerer, Martin. *Memory and Hypnotic*

Age Regression. International Univ. Press, Lido Beach, N.Y., 1959.

Reiser, Morton F. *Mind, Brain, Body.* Basic Books, New York, 1984.

Rendel, Peter. *The Chakras.* Samuel Weiser Inc., New York, 1979.

Restak, Richard M., M.D. *The Brain.* Bantam Books, New York, 1984.

Restak, Richard M., M.D. *The Mind.* Bantam Books, New York, 1988.

Reyes, Benito F. *Conscious Dying.* World Univ. of America, Ojai, Calif., 1986.

Ring, Kenneth. *Heading Toward Omega.* William Morrow & Co., New York, 1984.

Ring, Kenneth. *Life at Death.* Quill, New York, 1982.

Ring, Kenneth. *The Omega Project.* William Morrow & Co., New York, 1992.

Ritchie, George G., Jr., M.D. *My Life After Dying.* Hampton Roads Pub. Co., Hampton Roads, Va., 1991.

Roberts, Royston M. *Serendipity.* John Wiley & Sons, New York, 1989.

Rogo, D. S. *The Return From Silence: A Study of Near-Death Experiences.* Aquarian Press, England, 1989.

Roll, William G., et al. *Research in Parapsychology.* The Scarecrow Press, Metuchen, N.J., 1983.

Rorty, Richard. *Philosophy and the Mirror of Nature.* Princeton Univ. Press., N.J., 1979.

Rothenberg, Gerome, ed. *Technicians of the Sacred.* Anchor Books, New York, 1968.

Sabom, Michael B., M.D. *Recollections of Death.* Harper & Row, New York, 1982.

Sagan, Carl. *The Dragons of Eden.* Ballantine Books, New York, 1977.

Schrodinger, Erwin. *My View of the World.* Ox Bow Press, Woodbridge, Conn., 1964.

Schrodinger, Erwin. *What Is Life?* Cambridge University Press, Mass., 1967.

Schrodinger, Erwin. *My View of the World.* Ox Bow Press, Woodbridge, Conn., 1983.

Schwartz, Leni. *The World of the Unborn.* Richard Marek Pub., New York, 1980.

Scully, Thomas, M.D., and Scully, Celia. *Playing God: The New World of Medical Choices.* Simon & Schuster, New York, 1987.

Sheets, Cook, Sarah. *Children and Dying.* Health Sciences Corp., New York, 1973.

Sheikh, Anees A. *Imagination and Healing.* Baywood Pub. Co., Amityville, N.Y., 1984.

Solfvin, G. F., and Roll, W. G. "A case of RSPK with an epileptic agent." In J.D. Morris and W.G. Roll, eds., *Research in Parapsychology.* Scarecrow Press, Metuchen, N.J., 1975.

Sorensen, Michele R., and Willmore, David R. *The Journey Beyond Life.* Family Affair Books, 1988.

Stack, Rick. *Out of Body Adventures.* Contemporary Books, New York, 1988.

Swain, Jasper. *On the Death of My Son.* Aquarian Press, England, 1974.

Tart, Charles T., ed. *Altered States of Consciousness Revised and Updated.* Harper, San Francisco, 1990.

Taylor, Gordon R. *The Natural History of the Mind.* Penguin Books, New York, 1979.

Thompson, C.J.S. *The Mystery and Lore of Apparitions.* Frederick A. Stokes Co., New York, 1974.

Villoldo, Alberto. *The Four Winds.* Harper & Row, New York, 1990.

von Franz, Marie-Louise. *On Dreams and Death.* Shambhala, Boston, 1987.

Weil, Andrew, M.D. *Health and Healing.* Houghton Mifflin Co., Boston, 1983.

Weiss, Brian L., M.D. *Many Lives, Many Masters.* Simon & Schuster, New York, 1988.

White, John. *A Practical Guide to Death and Dying.* Theosophical Pub. House, England, 1980

Whitton, Joel L., and Fisher, Joe. *Life Between Life.* Warner Books, New York, 1986.

Wilkerson, Ralph. *Beyond and Back.* Melody Land Productions, Anaheim, 1977.

Williams, Wendy. *The Power Within.* Simon & Schuster, New York, 1990.

Winson, Jonathan. *Brain and Psyche: The Biology of the Unconscious.* Vintage, New York, 1985.

Wixom, Hartt, and Wixom, Judene. *Trial By Terror.* Horizon Pubs., Bountiful, Utah, 1987.

Worden, J. William. *Grief Counseling and Grief Therapy.* Springer Publishing Co., New York, 1991.

Young, J. Z. *Philosophy and the Brain.* Oxford Univ. Press, New York, 1988.

Zaleski, Carol. *Other World Journeys.* Oxford University Press, New York, 1987.

Zukav, Gary. *The Dancing Wu Li Masters.* Bantam Books, New York, 1979.

SELECTED BIBLIOGRAPHY OF
PAPERS AND PERIODICALS

Bauer, Martin. "Near-Death Experiences and Attitude Change." *Anabiosis: the Journal for Near-Death Studies*, Spring 1985.

Bear, David M., and Fedio, Paul. "Quantitative Analysis of Interictal Behavior in Temporal Lobe Epilepsy." *Archives of Neurology* 34 (Aug 1977).

Becker, Carl B. "Views From Tibet: NDS and the Book of the Dead." *Anabiosis: the Journal for Near-Death Studies*, Spring 1985.

Benoliel, J.Q. "Death Influence in Clinical Practice: A Course for Graduate Students." *Death Education* 5 (1982): 327–55.

Blackmore, Susan. "Are Out-of-Body Experiences Evidence for Survival?" *Anabiosis: the Journal for Near-Death Studies*, Dec. 1983.

Blackmore, Susan. "Visions from the dying brain/Near-Death experiences may tell us more about consciousness and the brain than about what lies beyond the grave." *New Scientist*, May 5, 1988.

Blackmore, Susan J., and Troscianko, Tom S. "The Physiology of the Tunnel." *Journal of Near-Death Studies*, Fall 1989.

Botkin, Jeffrey, M.D. "Making Decisions About Resuscitation in Children." *Medical Ethics: for the Pediatrician* 6, no. 3 (July 1991).

Braun, Bennett G., M.D. "Towards a Theory of Multiple Personality and Other Dissociative Phenomena." *Psy-

chiatric Clinics of North America 7, no. 1 (March 1984).

Byl, P. "The Near-Death Experience." *Kansas Nurse* 63, no. 7 (1988).

Cahill, Susan. "Trapped in Living Death/The Agonizing Dilemmas of High-Tech Life Support." Outlook Commentary and Opinion, *The Washington Post*, Aug. 12, 1990.

Comer, N.L., Madow, L., and Dixon, J.J. "Observations of Sensory Deprivation in a Life-Threatening Situation." *Am. J. Psychiatry* 124 (1967): 164–69.

Corcoran, D.K. "Helping Patients Who've Had Near-Death Experiences." *Nursing* November, 1988, 34–39.

Counts, Dorothy Ayers. "Near-Death and Out-of-Body Experiences in a Malasian Society." *Anabiosis: the Journal for Near-Death Studies*, Dec. 1983.

Coxon, Valerie Jean. "Subjective Perceptions of the Demands of Hospitalization and Anxiety in Bone Marrow Transplant Patients." Ph.D. thesis, Univ. of Washington, 1989.

Dickinson, G. E., and Pearson, A. A. "Differences in Attitudes toward Terminal Patients among Selected Medical Specialties of Physicians." *Medical Care* 17, no. 6 (1979): 682–85.

Ehrenwald, J. "A Neurophysiological Model of Psi Phenomena." *J. of Nerv. and Ment. Dis.* 154 (1972): 406–18.

Ehrenwald, J. "Cerebral Localization and the Psi Syndrome." *J of Nerv. and Ment. Dis.* 161, no. 6 (1975): 393–98.

Feifel, H., Hanson, S., and Jones, R., et al. "Physicians Consider Death." *Proceedings of the American Psychological Association* 2 (1967): 201–202.

Fitts, W. T., and Ravdin, I. S. "What Philadelphia Physicians Tell Patients with Cancer." *JAMA* 153 (1953): 901–904.

Freeman, C. "Near-Death Experiences: Implications for Medical Personnel." *Occupational Health Nursing Newsletter* 33, no. 7: 349–59.

Friedman, H. "Physician Management of Dying Patients." *Psychiatry in Medicine* 1 (1970): 295–305.

Gabbard, G. O., Twemlow, S. W. "Do Near-Death Experiences Occur Only Near Death? Revisited." *Journal of Near-Death Studies* 10, no. 1 (Fall 1991).

Gabbard, G. O., Twemlow, S. W., and Jones, F. C., "Do Near-Death Experiences Occur Only Near Death?" *Journal of Nervous and Mental Disease* 169 (1981): 374–77.

Georgeson, Mark A., and Harris, Michael G. "Apparent foveofugal drift of counterphase gratings." *Perception and Psychophysics* 7 (1978): 527–36.

Greeley, Andrew. "The Paranormal Is Normal: A Sociologist Looks at Parapsychology." *Univ. of Arizona NORC*, 1975.

Greyson, B. "Increase in psychic phenomena following near-death experiences." *Theta.* 11 (1983): 26–29.

Greyson, Bruce, M.D. "A Typology of Near-Death Experiences." *Am. J. Psychiatry* 142 (Aug. 1985): 8.

Gruen, Arno. "The Relationship of Sudden Infant Death and Parental Unconscious Conflicts." *Pre- and Peri-Natal Psychology Journal*, 1987.

Heim, A. "Notizen ueber den Ton durch Absturz." *Jahrb. Schweiz Alpenklub* 27 (1882): 327.

Herzog, D. B., and Herrin J. T. "Near-Death Experiences in the Very Young." *Crit. Care. Med.* 13, no 12 (1985), 1074–75.

Horrax, Gilbert, M.D. "Visual Hallucinations as a Cerebral Localizing Phenomenon." *Archives of Neurology and Psychiatry.*

"How the Medical Staff Copes with Dying Patients: A Critical Review." *Omega* 7, no. 1 (1976): 11–21.

Irwin, H. J. "Out of Body Experiences and Attitudes to Life and Death." *Journal of the American Society for Psychical Research* 82 (1988): 237–51.

Irwin, H. J. "The Psychological Function of Out-of-Body Experiences. So Who Needs the Out-of-Body Experience?" *J. of Nerv. and Ment. Dis.* 169, no. 4 (1981): 244–48.

Irwin, Harvey. "The Near-Death Experience in Childhood." *Australian Parapsychological Review* no. 14 (1989).

Jansen, K. "Near-Death Experience and the NMDA Receptor." *British Medical Journal* 298 (1989): 6689.

Jansen, K. "Neuroscience and the Near-Death Experience: Roles for the NMSA-PCP Receptor, the Sigma Receptor and the Endopsychosins." *Med. Hypotheses* 31, no. 1 (1990): 25–29.

Jansen, K.L.R. "Neuroscience and the Near-Death Experiences: Roles for the Capital NMSA-PCP Receptor, the Sigma Receptor and the Endopsychosins." *Medical Hypotheses*, 1990.

Kandel, Eric R., and Schwartz, James H. "Molecular Biology of Learning: Modulation of Transmitter Release." *Science* 218 (October 1982): 29.

Kohr, R. "Near-Death Experiences and its relationship to psi and various altered states. *Theta* 10 (1982): 50–53.

Kohr, Richard L. "Near-Death Experiences, Altered States, and PSI Sensitivity." *Anabiosis: the Journal for Near-Death Studies*, Dec. 1983.

Kubie, Lawrence S., M.D. "Some Implications for Psychoanalysis of Modern Concepts of the Organization of the Brain." *Psychoanal. Quart.* 22 (1958).

Littlefield, C., and Fleming, S. "Measuring Fear of Death: A Multidimensional Approach." *Omega* 15 (2) (1984–85): 131–38.

Locke, T. P., and Shontz, F. C. "Personality Correlates of the Near-Death Experience: A Preliminary Study." *Journal of the American Society for Psychical Research* 77 (1983): 311–318.

Lown, Bernard, M.D., et al. "Psychophysiologic Factors in Sudden Cardiac Death." *American Journal of Psychiatry* 137 (Nov. 1980): 11.

McPhee, A. T. "Kids Who Almost Died." *Current Science* 76, no. 9 (Jan. 1991): 4–5.

Mahl, G. F. Rothenberg, A., Delgado, J.M.R., et al. "Psychological Responses in the Human to Intracerebral Electrical Stimulation." *Psychosomatic Medicine* 26, no. 4 (1964): 337–68.

Mandell, A. "Nurses' Feelings About Working with the Dying." *American Journal of Nursing* 81, no. 6 (1981): 1194–97.

Mesulam, M. "Dissociative States With Abnormal Temporal Lobe EEG." *Archives of Neurology* 38 (March 1981): 176–81.

Mesulam, Marsel, M.D. "Dissociative States with Abnormal Temporal Lobe EEG: Multiple Personality and the Illusion of Possession." *Archives of Neurology* 38 (March 1981).

Moody, R. J. "Near-Death Experiences: Dilemma for the Clinician." *Va. Med.* 104, no. 10: 687–90.

Moreno, Jonathan D. "Is Life-Prolonging Treatment Always in a Child's Best Interest?" *Medical Ethics: for the Pediatrician* 6, no. 1 (Jan. 1991).

Morse, M. L. "A Near-Death Experience in a Seven-Year-Old Child." *American Journal of Diseases of Children.* Vol 127: 951–61, 1983.

Morse, M. L., Castillo, P., Venecia, D. et al. "Childhood Near-Death Experiences." *American Journal of Diseases of Children* 140 (1986): 1110–13.

Morse, M. L., Connor, D., and Tyler, D. "Near-Death Experiences in a Pediatric Population." *AJDC* 139 (1985): 595–600.

Morse, M. L., Neppe, V. "Near-Death Experiences" (letter) *Lancet*, April 6, 1991, p. 386.

Morse, Melvin L., M.D., et al. "Near-Death Experiences: A Neurophysiological Explanatory Model." *Journal of Near-Death Studies*, Fall 1989.

Mount, B., Jones, A., and Patterson, A. "Death and Dying Attitudes in a Teaching Hospital." *Urology* 4 (1974): 741–47.

Mullan, Sean, M.D., and Penfield, Wilder, M.D. "Illusions of Comparative Interpretation and Emotion." *Archives of Neurology and Psychiatry* 81 (March 1959).

Negovsky, V. A. "Postresuscitation disease." *Crit Care Med.* 16, no. 10 (1988): 942–46.

Negovsky, Vladimir A., M.D. "Postresuscitation Disease." *Critical Care Medicine* (USSR Medical Sciences), 1988.

Nelson, G. K. "Preliminary Study of the Electroencephalograms of Mediums." *Parapsychologica* 4 (1970): 30–35.

Neppe, V. M. "Subjective Paranormal Experience." *Psi-M* 2, no. 3 (1980): 2–3.

Neppe, V. M. "Subjective Paranormal Experience and

Temporal Lobe Symptomatology." *Parapsychological J. of S.A.* 1, no. 2 (1980): 99–101.

Neppe, V. M. "Symptomatology of Temporal Lobe Epilepsy." *SA Medical Journal* 62, no. 5 (Dec. 1981): 9023–9073.

Neppe, V. M. "Temporal Lobe Symptomatology in Subjective Paranormal Experiences." *J. Amer. Soc. Psych. Res.* 77, no. 1 (1983): 1–29.

Neppe, Vernon M. "Temporal Lobe Symptomatology in Subjective Paranormal Experiences." *The Journal of the American Society for Psychical Research* 77, no. 1 (Jan. 1983).

Noyes, R. J. "Attitude change following near-death experiences." *Psychiatry* 43, no 3 (1980): 234–42.

Noyes, R., Jr. "The Human Experience of Death or, What Can We Learn from Near-Death Experiences?" *Omega* 13 (3) (1982–83): 251–59.

Olson, M. "The Out-of-Body Experience and Other States of Consciousness." *Archives of Psychiatr. Nurs.* 1, no. 3 (1987); 201–7.

Olson, Melodie. "The Out-of-Body Experience and Other States of Consciousness." *Archives of Psychiatric Nursing* 1, no. 3 (June 1987): 201–7.

Owens, J. E., Cook, E. W., and Stevenson, I. "Features of Near-Death Experience in Relation to Whether or not Patients Were Near Death." *Lancet* 336 (1990): 1175–77.

Palmer, J., and Dennis, M. "A Community Mail Survey of Psychic Experiences." *J. Am. Soc. Psychical Research* 73, no. 3 (1979): 221–51.

Parisha, S., and Stevenson, I. "Near-death experiences in India." *J. of Nerv. and Ment. Dis.* 174, no. 3: 165–70.

The Pediatric Forum. "Explaining the Phenomena of Near-Death Experiences." *American Journal of Diseases of Children* 141 (Aug. 1987).

Penfield, W. "The Role of the Temporal Cortex in Certain Psychical Phenomena." *J. Ment Sci. 1955*; 101: 451–465.

Pilaczynska, E., and Rybakowski, J. "Experience of the OBE Type in a Patient with Schizophrenia." *Psychiatr. Pol.* 22, no. 2 (1988).

Pope, John E. "Near-Death Experiences and Attitudes Towards Life, Death and Suicide." Master's thesis, New England Univ., Armidale, Nov. 1991.

Punzak, Dan. "The Use of Near-Death Phenomena in Therapy." *Journal of Near-Death Studies*, Spring 1989.

Reker, G. T., and Peacock, E. J. "The Life Attitude Profile. A Multidimensional Instrument for Assessing Attitudes Towards Life." *Canadian Journal of Behavioral Science*. 13 (1981): 264–273.

Ricards, Phillip. "Visionary Mystical Experience: An Undervalued Type of Mystical Experience." *American Academy of Religion*, April 3, 1987.

Ring, K., and Franklin, S. "Do Suicide Survivors Report Near-Death Experiences?" *Omega: Journal of Death and Dying* 12 (1981–82): 191–208.

Ring, Kenneth, and Rosing, Christopher J. "The Omega Project: An Empirical Study of the NDE-Prone Personality." *Journal of Near-Death Studies*, Summer 1990.

Roberts, Glenn, and Owen, John. "The Near-Death Experience." *British Journal of Psychiatry* 153 (1988): 607–617.

Rosen, D. H. "Suicide survivors. A Follow-up Study of Persons Who Survived Jumping from the Golden Gate and San Francisco Bay Bridges." *Western Journal of Medicine* 122 (1975): 289–94.

Rosen, D. H. "Suicide Survivors: Psychotherapeutic implications of egocide." *Suicide and Life-threatening Behavior* 6 (1976): 209–15.

Sabom, M. B. "The Near-Death Experience" (letter) *JAMA* 244, no. 1 (1980): 29–30.

Sabom, M. B., and Kreutizer S. "Near-death experiences" (letter) *New England Journal of Medicine* 297, no. 19 (1977).

Sabom, M. B., and Kreutiziger, S. "Near-Death Experiences" *J. Fla. Med. Assoc.* 64, no. 9 (1977): 648–50.

Schenk, Laura, and Bear, David, M.D. "Multiple Personality and Related Dissociative Phenomena in Patients with Temporal Lobe Epilepsy." *Am. J. Psychiatry* 138 (October 1981): 10.

Schleifer, Steven J., M.D., et al. "Suppression of Lymphocyte Stimulation Following Bereavement." *JAMA* 250, no. 3 (July 15, 1983).

Schnapper, N. "The Psychological Implications of Severe Trauma: Emotional Sequelae to Unconsciousness." *J Trauma* 15 (1975): 94–95.

Schnaper, Nathan, M.D., and Panitz, Harriet. "Near Death Experiences: Perception Is Reality." *Journal of Near-Death Studies*, Winter 1990.

Schneidman, E. S. "On the Deromanticizing of Death." *American Journal of Psychotherapy* 25 (1971): 4–17.

Schoonmaker, F. "Denver Cardiologist Discloses Findings after 18 Years of Near-Death Research." *Anabiosis*, 1, no. 1 (1979): 1–2.

Schroter-Kunhardt, M. "Erfahrungen Sterbender wahrend des linischen Todes." pp. 1014–29. *Zeitschrift Fur Allgemeinmedizin*. 66. Jahrgang, Heft 35/36 20, December 1990.

Serdahely, W., Drenk, A., and Serdahely, J. J. "What Caregivers Need to Understand About the Near-Death Experience." *Geriatric Nursing* 9, no. 4 (1988): 238–41.

Serdahely, William J. "A Pediatric Near-Death Experience: Tunnel Variants." *Omega: Journal of Death and Dying*, 1989–90.

Serdahely, William J. "Why Near-Death Experiences Intrigue Us." *Journal of Near-Death Studies*, Spring 1989.

Serdahely, William J., and Walker, Barbara A. "The Near-Death Experience of a Nonverbal Person with Congenital Quadriplegia." *Journal of Near-Death Studies*, Winter 1990.

Solomon, George F., and Amkraut, Alfred A. "Psychoneuroendocrinological Effects on the Immune Response." *Ann. Rev. Microbiol* 35 (1981): 155–84.

Stevenson, Ian, et al. "Are Persons Reporting 'Near-Death Experiences' Really Near Death? A Study of Medical Records." *Omega: Journal of Death and Dying*, 1989–90.

Stevenson, I., and Greyson, B. "Near-Death Experiences, Relevance to the Question of Survival after Death." *JAMA* 242, no. 3 (1979): 265–67.

Stumpfe, K. D. "Psychosomatic Reactions to the Experience of Near Death. A State of Affective Dissociation." *Z Psychosom Med Psychoanal* 31, no. 3 (1985): 215–25.

Sutherland, C. "The Near-Death Experience. Claiming Life for the First Time." *Pallicom* 8 (1988): 18–23.

Sutherland, C. "Psychic Phenomena Following Near-Death Experiences. An Australian Study." *Journal of Near-Death Studies* 8 (1989): 93–103.

Telling, W.H.M. "The Value of Psychical Research to the Physician." *J. Ment. Sci.* (1928) 74:634–648.

Templer, D. I. "The Construction and Validation of a Death Anxiety Scale. *Journal of General Psychology* 82 (1970): 165–77.

Tobacyk, J. J., and Mitchell, T. P. "The Out-of-Body Experience and Personality Adjustment." *J. of Nerv. and Mental Dis.* 175, no. 6 (1987): 367–70.

Trevelyan, J. "Near-Death Experiences." *Nursing Times* 85, no. 28 (1989): 39–41.

Tucker, G. J., and Neppe, V. M. "Neurology and Psychiatry: Critical Review and Update." *General Hospital Psychiatry* 10, 24–33 1988.

Tucker, G. J., Price, T.R.P., Johnson, V.B., et al. "Phenomenology of Temporal Lobe Dysfunction: A Link to Atypical Psychosis." *Journal of Nervous and Mental Disease* 174, no. 6 (1986): 348–56.

Twemlow, S. W., Gabbard, G. O., and Jones, F. C. "The out-of-body experience. A Phenomenological Typology Based on Questionnaire Responses." *Am. J. Psychiatry* 139, no. 4 (1982): 450–55.

Ullman, M., and Krippner, S. "An Experimental Approach to Dreams and Telepathy: A Report of Three Studies." *Amer. J. Psychiatry* 126, no 9 (March 1970): 1282–89.

Walker, Barbara A., and Serdahely, William J. "Historical Perspectives on Near-Death Phenomena." *Journal of Near-Death Studies*, Winter 1990.

Walker, F. O. "A Nowhere Near-Death Experience. Heavenly Choirs Interrupt Myelography." (letter) *JAMA* 261, no. 22 (1989): 3245–46.

White, Robert L., M.D., and Liddon, Sim C., M.D. "Ten Survivors of Cardiac Arrest." *Psychiatry in Medicine* (Univ. of Virginia) 3 (1972).

CLOSER TO THE LIGHT

by

MELVIN MORSE

Available at bookstores everywhere.
Published by Ivy Books.